SMART MON

GRADE 6 & 7 FINANCIAL LITERACY

Empower Your 11 & 12 Year Olds with Essential Money Skills

AUTHOR

DIANE POPE

Copyright Page

Title: Smart Money Lessons for Kids: Grade 6 & 7 Financial Literacy

Sub Title: Empower Your 11 & 12 Year Olds with Essential Money Skills

Written By: Diane Pope

Created and Published by Skilled Fun

For permission requests, contact the creator & publisher:

Skilled Fun

401 Ryland Street,

Suite 200-A,

Reno, NV, 89502,

USA

ISBN: 979-8-89256-033-7

Printed in USA

CONTENTS

SPECIAL BONUS

Want this bonus book for free?

SKILLS and be the first to claim a free download of our upcoming releases.

Scan the QR CODE

Join Today!

INTRODUCTION

If I could go back in time and teach myself how to care for my money…

Oh, I would be so rich.

And it is not only about being rich either. It is about knowing the most important part of everyday life. Your house, your job, how many cars you can buy, can you eat out at McDonald's every day? Everything is decided by how much money you can make, save, and spend. Schools teach us algebra, geometry, and what Shakespeare said a couple of hundred years ago, but they somehow forget to teach us what to do with our money in an ever-changing world…

I remember, when I was growing up, we had cents and dollars that we could split into coins, but now it is nothing like that. You have online cash transactions like Apple Pay, etc. You have to make a bank account as soon as you turn 18 so you can get a nice job and take out money from ATMs. No one told you how all of this works, so you never know what banking fees are, or what is your best option. Don't even get me started on insurance and what scams are.

It took me twenty years to learn all of that by myself, but I am going to make this easier on you by breaking down everything as simply as I can.

What do you have to do?

Nothing much, just keep reading!

1

THE ADVANCED WORLD OF SMART MONEY

See, in the world of today, you do not only have to have money, but you also have to understand the concept of "smart money."

So let me formally welcome you, young explorers, to the intriguing world of Smart Money!

This chapter marks the beginning of an exciting adventure where we'll uncover the secrets of money and learn why it's so important in our lives.

Picture money as a special tool that helps us get the things we need and want. It's like a magical key that opens doors to a world of possibilities. From buying toys to saving up for a new bike, money plays a big role in making our dreams come true.

Now, let's go back in time and explore the history of money. It wasn't always coins and bills; people used to trade goods like shells or livestock. Imagine trying to buy your favorite snacks with seashells today—it would be quite a challenge! Thankfully, money has evolved, and we now have coins, bills, and even digital forms like credit cards.

Is all of this economics?

Economics might sound like a big word, but it's all about how people make and trade things to meet their needs. Think of it as a giant puzzle where everyone plays a part. Money, our trusty sidekick, helps us solve this puzzle by making it easier to exchange what we have for what we want.

Being smart with money isn't about having a magic wand; it's about making wise choices. Imagine you have a jar of marbles—each marble represents a choice you make with your money. You can use them to buy a toy now or save them up for a bigger, cooler toy later. This chapter sets the stage for becoming a money maestro, where you learn to juggle your marbles wisely.

Why does being smart with money matter? Well, it helps us achieve our goals and dreams. Whether it's buying a new video game or saving up for a family trip, money is the key to turning dreams into reality. By understanding the value of money, we can make it work for us, like a helpful friend guiding us through the twists and turns of life.

Now that we've laid the groundwork for our journey into the world of Smart Money, let's take a closer look at how money has changed over time and the different forms it can take.

Our adventure through the history of money continues! As we know, in the early days, people used to trade goods directly. Imagine swapping your toy car for a friend's action figure—that's a form of trade. However, as communities grew, this direct trading became a bit tricky. So, people got creative. They started using special items, like shiny stones or rare feathers, as a middle step in trading. These special items became a kind of "stand-in" for the things people wanted.

Eventually, societies realized that using something widely accepted as valuable made trading even easier. And voila! Money, in the form of coins and later paper bills, was born. Now, think about your favorite snack or game. Instead of trading toys or shells, you can hand over a few dollars, and it's yours!

Money makes trading smoother and helps everyone get what they need.

Coins and bills are like the superheroes of the money world. They come in different shapes, sizes, and colors, each with a special job. The small coins—like pennies, nickels, dimes, and quarters—are like the sidekicks, helping us with everyday purchases. Bills, on the other hand, are the big heroes, tackling larger transactions. You might have seen a one-dollar bill, five-dollar bill, or even a twenty-dollar bill.

Imagine going to a store with a bunch of coins and bills in your pocket. You're ready to conquer the world of buying and trading! These coins and bills are your allies in the world of Smart Money, helping you make choices and turn your marbles into real treasures.

Our adventure doesn't stop with coins and bills. In today's world, we also have digital money. It's like having invisible coins and bills that live inside computers and phones. Have you heard of credit cards or digital wallets? These are tools that let us use our digital money to buy things without touching a single coin or bill.

Imagine you're shopping online for a new game. With a click here and a tap there, your digital money moves from your account to the game store's account. It's quick and easy, like magic! But remember, just like with coins and bills, we need to be smart about using digital money. Our digital tools are powerful, but it's up to us to use them wisely.

Now that you know about the different forms of money, think of them as tools in your Smart Money toolkit. Coins, bills, and digital money are like magical instruments helping you navigate the world of buying and selling. As we move forward in our adventure, we'll learn how to use these tools wisely, making every choice count.

Here is a table that will help you understand smart money in a jiffy:

Aspect	**Coins and Bills**	**Digital Money**
Form	Physical: Metal (coins), Paper (bills)	Digital: Exists electronically in computers and phones
Examples	- Pennies, nickels, dimes, quarters	- Credit cards
	- One, five, twenty-dollar bills	- Digital wallets (like PayPal, Apple Pay)
Usage	Everyday transactions (snacks, small items)	Online purchases, electronic transactions
Portability	Easily carried in pockets or wallets	No physical presence, stored on devices

Visibility	Tangible and visible	Virtual, no physical representation
Exchange Medium	Often used for direct transactions	Acts as a mediator in electronic transactions
Transaction Speed	Slower compared to digital transactions	Quick and efficient
Limitations	Limited denominations for larger purchases	Requires responsible use to avoid overspending
Accessibility	Widely accepted, especially in physical stores	Essential for online shopping and digital transactions
Physical Handling	Prone to wear and tear	No physical handling, less risk of damage

Our journey into the advanced world of Smart Money is just getting started. In the upcoming chapters, we'll dive into the exciting realms of earning money, budgeting like a pro, and discovering the superpower of saving. So, young adventurers, get ready to unlock more secrets and become true Smart Money experts!

2

MONEY BEYOND BASICS: MASTERING ADVANCED CURRENCY CONCEPTS

Imagine you've already mastered the basics of coins, bills, and digital money. Now, let's venture into the more sophisticated aspects of currency, where we'll uncover the secrets of advanced money management.

Have you ever wondered why money from one country looks different from another? That's because each country has its own currency. When you travel to another place, you might need to exchange your local money for the currency of the country you're visiting. It's like trading marbles for shells but on a global scale!

Exchange rates are like the magical numbers that determine the value of one currency compared to another. For example, if you're in the United States and want to exchange dollars for euros to buy something in Europe, you'll need to know the exchange rate. Understanding this concept helps you make smart choices when dealing with international transactions.

Hold on to your hats, because we're about to enter the digital frontier of money—cryptocurrency! Unlike coins and bills, cryptocurrencies are entirely digital and use encryption techniques to secure transactions. Bitcoin, Ethereum, and other cryptocurrencies might sound like words from a futuristic movie, but they are real and changing the way we think about money.

As you become more of a world traveler (or dream of becoming one), it's essential to know how to handle different currencies. Here are a few smart tips:

- Research exchange rates before your trip.
- Be aware of fees when exchanging money.
- Understand the value of the currency you're using.

Now, let's talk about making your money work for you. Investments are like planting seeds that grow into money trees over time. We'll introduce you to simple investment concepts suitable for your age, sparking the idea that your money can do more than just sit in a piggy bank.

Have you ever heard the saying, "Money makes money"? Interest is the secret sauce that makes this happen. When you save or invest your money, banks or investment platforms might pay you a little extra, called interest. It's like a reward for letting your money hang out with them.

As you venture into these advanced currency concepts, remember that becoming a Smart Money expert is a journey. We've now equipped you with the knowledge to navigate international transactions, understand the digital frontier of cryptocurrency, and plant the seeds for future financial growth.

Now that we've delved into the advanced realms of currency exchange, cryptocurrencies, and the fascinating world of investments, let's continue our exploration of Smart Money with a deeper dive into earning money, setting financial goals, and the magic of compound interest.

Earning money isn't just about receiving it; it's also about discovering your skills and passions. As you grow older, opportunities to earn money will arise. Whether it's through chores, part-time jobs, or even starting a small business, each opportunity teaches valuable lessons about responsibility, hard work, and the joy of earning.

Imagine having a treasure map leading you to your dream destination. Setting financial goals is like creating your own treasure map for life. It could be saving for a new game, a special toy, or even a future adventure. Learning to set and achieve these goals is a powerful skill that will stay with you throughout your life.

Now, prepare to be amazed by the magic of compound interest! It's like planting a money seed that grows into a giant money tree over time. When you save or invest your money, compound interest makes it grow faster. It's the reason why starting to save early is so powerful—your money earns interest on the interest!

As you become more familiar with advanced currency concepts, it's crucial to make smart choices with your money. Here are a few tips to guide you:

- Differentiate Between Needs and Wants: Understand what you truly need versus what you simply want.
- Budget Wisely: Keep track of your earnings and spending to ensure your money is working toward your goals.
- Save for the Future: Consider opening a savings account to watch your money grow with the help of compound interest.
- Learn From Mistakes: Everyone makes money mistakes. Use them as lessons to become even smarter with your finances.

Consider starting a Smart Money journal where you record your financial goals, earnings, and expenses. It's like having a diary for your money adventures, helping you stay on track and celebrate your successes.

In the upcoming chapters, we'll dive into the exciting world of entrepreneurship. Ever dreamed of starting your own business, big or small? We'll guide you through the steps, from brainstorming ideas to bringing them to life. Get ready to unleash your inner entrepreneur and discover how money can be a tool for creativity and innovation.

Our journey into the advanced world of Smart Money continues. Stay curious, stay eager, and get ready for the thrilling adventures that lie ahead, young money explorers!

3

FINANCIAL INDEPENDENCE: EMPOWERING YOUNG SPENDERS

Welcome, budding financial experts! In this chapter, we're delving into the concept of financial independence—a superpower that empowers you to make smart choices with your money and set the stage for a secure and exciting future.

Financial independence is like having your own set of wings. It means having enough money to cover your needs and pursue your goals without relying on others. As young spenders, the journey toward financial independence begins with understanding the value of money and making informed choices.

Budgeting isn't just for adults; it's a tool that can empower young spenders like you. Imagine your money as a team of superheroes, each with its own role. A budget helps you assign jobs to your money, ensuring it works together efficiently. From saving for that dream toy to setting aside money for future goals, budgeting is your secret weapon.

Earning money isn't just about getting pocket money; it's about setting and achieving goals. As you earn, consider dividing your money into categories—spending, saving, and sharing. This way, you're not just spending all your marbles at once. You're also planting seeds for future treasures through saving and contributing to others through sharing.

Do You know about the Power of Delayed Gratification?

Imagine you have a bag of candy, and you can choose to eat it all at once or save some for later. Delayed gratification is the ability to resist the temptation of immediate rewards for a bigger, more meaningful outcome in the future. It's a key skill in achieving financial independence—sacrificing a small treat today for a bigger, more satisfying reward tomorrow.

Being an empowered spender means making wise choices with your money. Here are some tips:

1. Prioritize Needs Over Wants:

Ensure your essential needs are met before spending on wants.

2.Comparison Shop:

Look for the best deals before making a purchase.

3.Quality Over Quantity:

Sometimes, it's better to invest in a high-quality item that lasts longer.

As young spenders, it's crucial to understand that money represents more than just coins and bills. It represents your effort, time, and choices. Every marble you earn and spend reflects your decisions, shaping your journey toward financial independence.

Challenge yourself to take small steps toward financial independence. It could be saving a portion of your pocket money, setting a goal for a special purchase, or finding creative ways to earn a little extra. Remember, financial independence is a journey, and every step you take brings you closer to your destination.

Get ready to experience the fulfillment that comes from using your money to create positive change.

Our journey into the world of Smart Money continues…

Now that you've started your journey towards financial independence, it's time to explore the fulfilling world of sharing and giving back. As you grow into a savvy spender, you'll realize that your ability to make a positive impact extends beyond personal goals to the well-being of others and the community.

Understanding Sharing:

Sharing is a wonderful way to connect with others and spread joy. It could be as simple as sharing a snack with a friend, lending a favorite book, or even helping a classmate with their homework. Through sharing, you not only strengthen your relationships, but also learn the importance of generosity and kindness.

Giving Back to the Community:

Financial independence isn't just about personal wealth; it's also about contributing to the greater good. As young spenders, you have the power to make a difference in your community. Consider participating in charity events, supporting local causes, or volunteering your time and skills. Your contributions, no matter how small, can create positive change.

Creating a Giving Plan:

Just like you budget for your spending and saving, consider creating a giving plan. Decide how much of your earnings you'd like to allocate for charitable contributions or community projects. It could be a percentage of your allowance, a set amount each month, or even the proceeds from a small business you've started.

The Ripple Effect of Positive Giving:

When you contribute to the well-being of others, you create a ripple effect of positivity. Your actions inspire those around you, fostering a sense of community and shared responsibility. Whether it's supporting a local animal shelter, planting trees, or helping those in need, your involvement makes a lasting impact.

Start Small:

You don't need a fortune to make a difference. Small, consistent efforts can lead to meaningful change.

Explore Causes You Care About:

Connect with causes that align with your interests and values. This makes giving more personal and rewarding.

Involve Friends and Family:

Encourage those around you to join in your efforts. Together, you can amplify the impact of your contributions.

As we wrap up this chapter on financial independence, remember that being a young spender isn't just about managing money for personal gain. It's about making choices that benefit not only yourself but also those around you. Financial independence empowers you to create a positive impact, setting the stage for a future where your Smart Money choices contribute to a better world.

In the upcoming chapters, we'll dive into the exciting world of entrepreneurship. Ever dreamed of starting your own business, big or small?

Let me create a basic plan for you to realize how you can use your power to become financially independent and responsible:

Week 1: Budgeting Adventure

Goal:

Create a simple budget for the month.

Activity:

- List your sources of income (allowance, chores, etc.).
- Identify three categories for your spending: Saving, Spending, and Sharing.
- Allocate a portion of your income to each category.
- Keep a physical or digital budgeting journal to track your allocations.

Week 2: Earning Exploration

Goal:

Explore new ways to earn money.

Activity:

- Brainstorm different ways you can earn extra money (extra chores, selling handmade crafts, etc.).
- Choose one earning activity to pursue during the month.
- Set a specific goal for how much you want to earn.

Week 3: Smart Spending Challenges

Goal:

Make wise spending choices.

Activity:

- Before making any purchases, compare prices and look for the best deals.
- Prioritize needs over wants—ask yourself if the purchase is necessary.
- Use the "30-Day Rule": If there's something you want, wait 30 days. If you still want it after that time, consider making the purchase.

Week 4: Sharing and Giving Back

Goal:

Contribute to your community through sharing and giving.

Activity:

- Identify a cause or charity you care about.
- Allocate a portion of your income to contribute to this cause.
- Explore volunteering opportunities in your community.

Throughout the Month: Financial Independence Journal

Goal:

Keep a record of your financial activities and experiences.

Activity:

- Use your budgeting journal to track your spending, saving, and sharing.
- Note any challenges you faced and how you overcame them.
- Celebrate your achievements and reflect on the impact of your financial choices.

Reflection and Adjustment (End of Month):

Goal:

Reflect on the month's financial journey and make adjustments.

Activity:

- Review your budget and assess how well you stuck to your allocations.
- Evaluate the success of your earning activity.

- Reflect on the joy and impact of your sharing and giving back initiatives.
- Adjust your budget for the next month based on your experiences and goals.

This monthly plan is designed to guide young spenders through various aspects of Smart Money, including budgeting, earning, spending wisely, and giving back to the community. The goal is to instill financial literacy skills while making the process enjoyable and educational.

Get ready to unleash your creativity and discover how your entrepreneurial spirit can turn dreams into reality. The journey of financial empowerment continues—stay enthusiastic, stay engaged, and get ready for the adventures that lie ahead, young financial trailblazers.

4

INVESTING INSIGHT: NAVIGATING THE WORLD OF INVESTMENTS

Ever wondered how your money could do more than just chill in your wallet or piggy bank? Well, get ready because we're about to dive into the exhilarating universe of investments! It's like a financial rollercoaster, but don't worry, we're here to make sure it's the fun kind.

Picture this: You're not just a student; you're an investor-in-training, making moves that could shape your financial future. In this chapter, we'll break down the mystery behind stocks, bonds, and the art of growing your money like a financial gardening pro.

So, grab your virtual financial binoculars because we're about to embark on an adventure into the world of Investing Insight. Get ready to explore, learn, and discover the magic that happens when your money starts working for you!

Investing is like planting seeds with the expectation that they will grow into mighty trees over time. Instead of just stashing money in a piggy bank, you're putting it to work in ways that have the potential to multiply. Investments come in various forms, and each offers a unique pathway to financial success.

The following are just some forms of investments you can think about right now:

1. Stocks: Owning a piece of a company makes you a shareholder. As the company grows, so does the value of your shares.
2. Bonds: Think of bonds as loans you provide to companies or the government. In return, you receive regular interest payments and the principal amount back when the bond matures.
3. Mutual Funds: These are like investment bundles that pool money from various investors to buy a diversified portfolio of stocks, bonds, or other securities.
4. Real Estate: Investing in properties can generate income through rent or appreciate in value over time.
5. Starting a Business: For those with an entrepreneurial spirit, investing in your own business can be a rewarding venture.

One of the most magical aspects of investing is compound growth. It's like a snowball effect where your money earns interest on the interest, creating a compounding effect that accelerates your wealth over time. Starting to invest early in high school gives you a significant advantage, as your money has more time to grow.

Investing involves a balance between risk and return. Generally, higher potential returns come with higher risk. It's crucial to understand your risk tolerance—how comfortable you are with the ups and downs of the market—and tailor your investment strategy accordingly.

This is how you create a middle school/high school investment plan:

Set Clear Goals:

Define your financial objectives—whether it's saving for college, a dream trip, or even early retirement.

Understand Risk Tolerance:

Assess how much risk you're willing to take. High-risk investments can offer high returns but may be more volatile.

Diversify Your Portfolio:

Don't put all your eggs in one basket. Spread your investments across different asset classes to minimize risk.

Stay Informed:

Keep an eye on market trends, economic news, and the performance of your investments. The more you know, the better decisions you can make.

Start Small:

You don't need a fortune to start investing. Many investment platforms allow you to begin with modest amounts.

Investing with Purpose:

Consider aligning your investments with your values. Sustainable and socially responsible investing allows you to support causes you care about while growing your wealth.

Investing is a journey of continuous learning. Don't be afraid to make mistakes—each one is a valuable lesson that contributes to your growth as an investor. Over time, you'll develop a keen understanding of the market and your own financial goals.

As you delve into the world of investments in middle school/high school, you're not just embracing the potential for financial growth; you're also cultivating valuable skills and perspectives that will serve you well in the future.

Investing is a crash course in financial literacy. Understanding concepts like stocks, bonds, and portfolios not only sharpens your financial acumen, but also positions you as a proactive participant in the global economy. It's a hands-on education that goes beyond the classroom.

Investing in stocks or even starting your own business introduces you to the entrepreneurial mindset. You'll learn to spot opportunities, analyze risks, and make informed decisions—skills that extend far beyond the world of finance. This mindset becomes a foundation for innovation and resilience.

Investing in middle school/high school is a strategic move toward securing your financial future. Whether you're eyeing your dream college, planning a business venture, or setting the stage for early retirement, your investment portfolio becomes a powerful tool for long-term financial planning.

Investing when you're in middle school and high school exposes you to the dynamics of the economy. You'll witness how global events, technological advancements, and shifts in consumer behavior can impact financial markets. This real-world experience hones your ability to adapt and make sound financial decisions in a constantly evolving landscape.

Staying informed about your investments requires you to be in tune with industry trends. This connection to real-world developments fosters a deeper understanding of the sectors you invest in, providing insights that go beyond mere financial gains.

As a middle school/high school investor, you have the potential to contribute to positive change. Consider investing in companies that align with your values—those committed to environmental sustainability, social responsibility, or ethical business practices. Your investments can become a force for good.

Engage with fellow middle school/high school investors, share insights, and learn from one another. Whether through investment clubs, online forums, or discussions with peers, collaborative learning enriches your investment journey and broadens your perspective.

Keep a meticulous record of your investments. Regularly assess your portfolio's performance, understand the factors influencing its growth, and use this data to refine your investment strategy. This practice instills discipline and sharpens your analytical skills.

As the school year concludes, take time to reflect on your investment journey. Consider the lessons learned, challenges faced, and successes achieved. Use this reflection to adjust your investment plan, set new goals, and refine strategies for the upcoming year.

5

MASTERING BUDGETING: CREATING A PERSONAL SPENDING PLAN

Picture yourself as the captain of your financial ship, navigating the seas of income and expenses with skill and precision. Are you ready to become the commander of your financial destiny? Let's set sail into the world of Mastering Budgeting!

Budgeting is like having a treasure map for your money. It's not about restricting yourself; it's about creating a plan that helps you achieve your goals while ensuring smooth sailing through the waves of income and spending. Your budget is your trusty compass guiding you toward financial success.

The first step in mastering budgeting is to map out your financial territory. List all your sources of income, whether it's an allowance, money from a part-time job, or even the occasional birthday gift. Every coin and bill that enters your treasure chest counts!

Now, let's embark on a journey of self-discovery. Track your spending for a month and categorize it into different buckets. This isn't about judgment; it's about understanding where your marbles are going. Are they mostly rolling towards snacks, gadgets, or perhaps saving up for a grand adventure?

Every captain needs a trusty toolbox, and your budgeting toolkit is no different. Here are the essential tools you'll use:

- Income Sheet: Where you list all the ways money comes into your life.
- Expense Tracker: Your map to categorize and track where your marbles are going.
- Goal Setting: The compass that points you in the direction of your dreams.

Setting Sail with Categories:

Divide your spending into categories like Saving, Spending, and Sharing. This not only helps you allocate your marbles wisely but also adds a touch of organization to your treasure chest.

Smart Goals:

Now, let's plot your course. Set SMART goals—Specific, Measurable, Achievable, Relevant, and Time-bound. Whether it's saving for a new video game, a weekend outing, or even contributing to a charity, your goals will become the North Star guiding your financial journey.

Navigating Challenges:

Every captain faces storms, and your budgeting adventure is no different. Unexpected expenses might pop up, but fear not! Having an emergency fund—a stash of marbles reserved for unexpected storms—will keep your ship sailing smoothly.

Reflecting on Your Journey:

As you sail through the month with your budgeting map, take time to reflect. Did you reach your goals? What challenges did you face, and how can you navigate them better next time? Reflection is the wind in your sails, propelling you forward with newfound wisdom.

As your budgeting ship sails through the financial seas, it's time to add some wind to your sails. Let's explore advanced budgeting techniques and additional tools to ensure your journey remains smooth and enjoyable.

1. *Zero-Based Budgeting:*

Imagine every dollar as a crew member on your ship. With zero-based budgeting, you give each dollar a job—whether it's for spending, saving, or sharing. This ensures no dollar is left idle, contributing to the efficiency of your financial crew.

2. *Envelope System:*

Picture having different envelopes for various spending categories—snacks, entertainment, saving, etc. Once an envelope is empty, you're done spending in that category for the month. It's a tangible way to control your spending and make informed choices.

3. *Percentage Budgeting:*

Allocate a percentage of your income to different categories. For example, 50% for needs (like snacks or school supplies), 30% for wants (like entertainment or gadgets), and 20% for savings or sharing. This method helps maintain a balanced financial ecosystem.

Here is what you have to do:

4. *Monthly Check-Ins:*

Schedule regular check-ins with your budgeting map. It's like giving your ship a quick maintenance check. Are you on course? Are there any adjustments needed? Checking in ensures you catch any unexpected financial storms before they become tempests.

5. *Adjusting the Sails:*

Your financial voyage is dynamic, and sometimes, you may need to adjust your sails. Life is full of changes—perhaps an increase in your allowance, a new part-time job, or unexpected expenses. Be flexible and tweak your budget accordingly.

Every successful captain knows the importance of celebrating victories. When you achieve a financial goal or overcome a budgeting challenge, celebrate it! Treat yourself to a little extra share of your favorite snack or acknowledge your accomplishment with a victory dance. Positive reinforcement keeps your financial crew motivated and excited about the journey ahead.

Think of your savings and investments as seeds planted in the fertile soil of your financial landscape.

Every successful garden starts with seeds, and in the financial world, those seeds are your savings. Start by setting aside a portion of your income in a savings account. This is your emergency fund, a safety net for unexpected storms. Remember, a well-nurtured savings garden provides peace of mind and financial security.

Now, let's sprinkle some investment magic into your garden. Investments are like specialized seeds that, with care and time, grow into mighty financial trees. Explore investment options like stocks, bonds, and mutual funds. Diversify your garden by planting a variety of seeds, spreading the risk, and ensuring a healthy, flourishing financial ecosystem.

Ever heard of compound interest? It's like the sunlight that makes your financial garden thrive. When you reinvest the interest your investments earn, it's added to the principal, creating a compound effect. Over time, this magical force accelerates the growth of your money garden, turning small seeds into substantial financial trees.

Just as you set goals for your budget, establish goals for your money garden. Want to save for a new gaming console, a dream vacation, or even future education? Your goals are the compass that guides your financial garden's growth. Break them down into achievable steps, making your journey more manageable and enjoyable.

Just keep this in mind:

Where is the money going to go?	% Allocation	Money Spent $
EARNINGS		
SAVE		
SPEND		
SHARE		

This table is here for you to fill by yourself. How much you get, you give, and you spend is your own decision. Do you!

But find the best formula for yourself…

Let me break down the categories for you:

Earnings: Write down the total amount of money you earn or receive. This is your starting point.

Save: Decide how much of your earnings you want to save. You can start with a small percentage, like 20% or 30%. Calculate the amount to save based on your total earnings.

Spend: Allocate a portion of your earnings for things you want or enjoy. This is your spending money. Adjust the percentage to fit your needs and calculate the amount accordingly.

Share: Decide on a percentage to contribute to sharing or giving back. This could be money you donate to charity or use to help others. Calculate the amount based on your total earnings.

Your financial garden needs regular inspections. Keep a close eye on your savings and investments, making adjustments as needed. Are there new seeds to plant? Has a financial storm affected your garden? Regular inspections ensure your money garden stays healthy and vibrant.

The best part of tending to your money garden? The harvest! When your savings and investments have grown, you can enjoy the fruits of your financial labor. Whether it's funding a dream project, supporting a cause you care about, or simply treating yourself to a well-deserved reward, the harvest is a celebration of your financial success.

6

MONEY IN MOTION: INTRODUCTION TO BANKING SERVICES

Ever wondered where your money goes when it's not in your piggy bank or wallet? That's where banks come into play. Picture banks as the headquarters for your money, a safe and bustling hub where your dollars get a chance to work, socialize, and grow.

Meet the superhero of banking services—the savings account! It's like a fortress for your money, keeping it safe while offering a little extra power called interest. Interest is like a reward your money earns just for hanging out in the bank. The longer it stays, the more it multiplies—talk about a superpower!

Now, let's talk about the sidekick—the checking account. This trusty companion is there for your everyday transactions. Whether you're buying your favorite snacks, getting the latest gadgets, or treating yourself to a movie, your checking account is right by your side, making transactions a breeze.

Have you ever seen those little machines called ATMs? They're like magical money minions that listen to your commands. Need cash for a quick treat or to impress your friends with your shopping spree? Just tap a few buttons, and voilà—your money minions deliver the goods!

What about those fancy cards our parents have?

Imagine having little cards in your pocket that hold the power of your money kingdom. Debit cards are like magical keys that let you access your checking account, making purchases or withdrawing cash. Credit cards, on the other hand, are like borrowed power—they let you spend money up to a limit, but be careful, or you might end up owing more than you planned!

Welcome to the digital frontier of banking! Online banking is like having a portal to your money kingdom right on your device. Check your balances, move money around, and even set goals—all at the click of a button. It's like having a personal financial wizard in your pocket!

Worried about the safety of your money kingdom? Fear not! The FDIC (Federal Deposit Insurance Corporation) is like the guardian angel of your deposits, ensuring that even if something happens to the bank, your money is protected up to a certain amount.

Ready for a mission?

Your challenge is to explore the possibility of opening your very own savings or checking account. Seek the guidance of your trusted adults, like parents or guardians, to help you embark on this exciting financial quest.

As our journey into the world of Money in Motion continues, it's time to unlock the secrets of credit—a powerful tool that can amplify your financial abilities. Imagine it as a magical spellbook filled with opportunities for growth, responsibility, and financial empowerment.

Credit is like a magic wand that allows you to borrow money for various purposes. Whether you dream of starting your own business, attending college, or owning a home, credit can be the key to turning those dreams into reality. But remember, wielding this magic wand comes with great responsibility.

The Credit Card Chronicles:

Enter the realm of credit cards—those enchanting pieces of plastic that hold the key to a world of purchasing power. When used wisely, credit cards can be your allies, offering convenience, security, and even rewards. But beware, misuse can cast a spell of debt, leading to financial challenges.

To harness the true power of credit, one must master the art of responsible spellcasting. Here are some fundamental principles:

Wield Your Magic Wisely:

Only use credit for necessities or planned expenses. Avoid impulsive spellcasting that may lead to unnecessary debt. Let's talk about using credit wisely—it's like casting spells in your magical adventure. Imagine credit as a powerful spell that you can use for important things or carefully planned adventures.

Think of needs like getting the magic potion ingredients you really need or attending a special wizard training school—those are good times to use your credit spell. But watch out for impulsive spellcasting! That's when you use credit for things you want in the moment, like a super cool gadget or extra snacks.

To be a smart wizard with credit, plan ahead. Decide which spells are really necessary and fit with your big wizard goals. Avoid using your credit spell on things that might create problems later, like having too much debt. Imagine making a magical map (budget) to plan where your spells (money) should go—this helps you avoid casting spells on things you don't really need.

Remember, using credit is like casting spells—do it wisely, and it'll help your magical journey. Use it without thinking, and you might end up in some tricky situations.

Master the Repayment Spell:

Every spell cast must be repaid. Pay your credit card balance in full each month to avoid the interest spell, which can quickly accumulate and turn friendly financial magic into a troublesome curse.

It is a crucial skill that ensures your magical financial adventures remain bright and trouble-free. Picture each financial transaction as a spell cast, and just like any spell, it must be repaid.

To maintain a harmonious balance in your magical kingdom, it's essential to pay your credit card balance in full each month. This isn't just a recommendation; it's a powerful incantation that shields you from the dark forces known as interest spells. Failure to fully repay your credit card balance can quickly lead to the accumulation of these interest spells, turning what was once friendly financial magic into a troublesome curse.

Here is how you can differentiate between credit and debit:

Feature	Credit	Debit
Definition	Money borrowed From the bank or lender	Money taken from your own account
Source of Funds	Borrowed money	Your own money
Usage	Make purchases now, pay later	Make purchases with available funds
Example	Credit card purchases, personal loans	Debit card purchases, ATM withdrawals
Interest	Typically charges interest if not paid in full by due date	No interest charges, but some fees may apply
Risk	Potential debt if not managed wisely	Limited to available funds in the account
Statements	Monthly statements showing transactions	Monthly statements showing transactions
Bank Involvement	Involves a bank or lending institution	Involves a bank or financial institution

Imagine interest spells as mischievous imps that grow in number the longer they linger. By paying your credit card balance in full, you dispel these imps, ensuring they have no opportunity to cast shadows on your financial realm. This practice not only safeguards your magical treasures but also preserves the integrity of your credit spell, allowing you to continue your financial adventures unburdened by unnecessary curses.

Take heed, young wizards, and make it a habit to check your spellbook (credit card statement) regularly. Ensure that every spell you cast is promptly repaid, transforming your financial journey into a tale of prosperity rather than a struggle against troublesome curses. As you hone your skills in the art of repayment, you'll find that your mastery of this spell becomes a powerful tool in maintaining the radiant magic of your financial kingdom. May your repayment spell always shine bright, dispelling any shadows that threaten the brilliance of your financial realm!

Guard Against Dark Forces (Identity Theft):

Protect your financial identity like a valuable treasure. Shield your personal information, use strong passwords, and regularly check your credit report to ensure no dark forces are trying to misuse your magic. Consider your personal information as a valuable treasure chest, and treat it with the utmost care. Never share your wand (credit card) details or potion ingredients (personal details) with strangers, as they may use this information to cast harmful spells.

Create mighty shields by using strong passwords for your online portals. Think of these passwords as magical incantations that only you, the rightful wizard, can recite. Combine numbers, symbols, and magical words to create a formidable barrier against unauthorized entry.

Regularly inspect your credit report—it's like a magical mirror that reflects the state of your financial kingdom. By reviewing it frequently, you can ensure that no dark forces have tampered with your spells or misused your magical identity. If you spot any suspicious activities or unfamiliar spells on your report, act swiftly to neutralize the threat.

In times of uncertainty, call upon the guardians of financial security, like the Credit Bureau Wizards, who can assist you in dispelling any dark forces that seek to harm your financial well-being. Remember, your financial identity is a treasure worth protecting, and by staying vigilant, you can maintain the integrity of your magical kingdom and continue your journey toward financial mastery.

Don't let your credit potion become too potent. Use credit wisely, and only borrow what you can comfortably repay. Too much debt can cast a shadow over your financial well-being.

Your credit spellbook isn't just about credit cards. Other spells include:

Student Loans:

A magical spell to fund your education. Just remember, it's an investment in your future. Envision your educational journey as an epic quest, with student loans as the mystical key that unlocks the gates to the vast kingdom of wisdom.

Your thirst for learning, like a grand quest, takes you on exciting trails of magical sciences, ancient histories, or the wonders of numbers. This quest is uniquely yours, and the student loan spell is the trusty wand that guides you through the academic landscapes.

Rather than waiting for a dragon's hoard of gold coins, the student loan spell empowers you to invest gradually in your education. It's like having a magical reserve that supports your journey through the castle of wisdom, where every chapter brings new insights and skills.

As you weave the spell of student loans, remember that this magical investment is a bridge to realizing your dreams and goals. Just like any grand adventure, your educational journey is a tapestry of experiences and discoveries, and the student loan sorcery is your companion on this enchanted quest for knowledge.

Car Loans:

A transportation spell to help you embark on your adventures. Choose a spell that aligns with your budget and needs. Picture your dream car as a fantastical chariot, and the car loan as your reliable wand. Instead of waiting for a treasure chest of gold coins, the car loan charm allows you to pay a little bit each month, turning your dream chariot into a reality faster than you might think. Think of it as casting a monthly enchantment—a portion for the actual chariot (called principal) and a dash of extra magic (interest) to keep the spell going strong. With every monthly enchantment, you're drawing closer to the day when you'll ride in your very own magical chariot, ready for all the adventures the enchanted roads have to offer!

Mortgage Magic:

The ultimate homeownership spell. Plan wisely and choose a spell that fits your long-term goals. Imagine your dream home as a magical castle, and the mortgage as your trusty wand. Instead of needing all the gold coins at once, the mortgage spell lets you pay a bit of your castle's price each month, turning a big dream into achievable steps. Picture it like mixing a special potion every month—a part for the actual castle (called principal) and a sprinkle of extra magic (interest). So, every time you make a potion payment, you're getting closer to fully owning your magical abode. It's a journey of turning your dream into reality, one spell at a time!

As you delve into the world of credit, remember that knowledge is your most potent spell. Learn the ins and outs of credit, stay vigilant against financial dark forces, and use your magical abilities responsibly.

7

ENTREPRENEURSHIP UNLEASHED: EXPANDING YOUR BUSINESS VENTURES

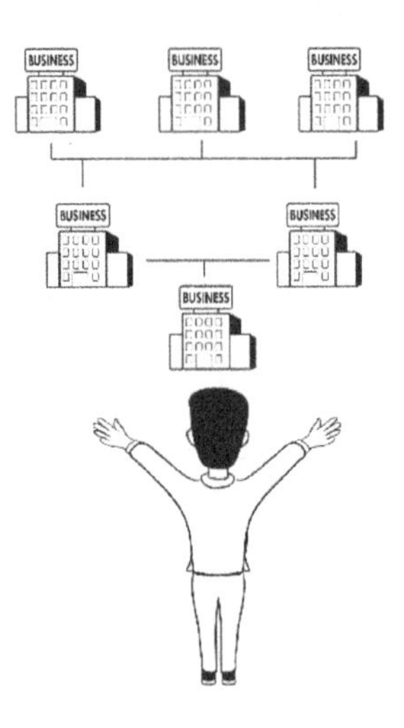

Welcome to the magical realms of entrepreneurship, where dreams become businesses, and businesses weave enchanting legacies. As we step into Chapter 9, we're about to dive into a spellbinding adventure. Get ready to unleash the magic that will shape the future stories told about your entrepreneurial journey.

Imagine this chapter as a treasure trove of wisdom, where you'll discover the secrets to crafting a legacy that echoes through the enchanted corridors of business history. It's time to don your entrepreneurial capes, wield your magical wands, and embark on a quest to leave an indelible mark on the magical world of business.

So, young business wizards, get ready for a journey filled with laughter, learning, and a sprinkle of entrepreneurial mischief. The Legacy Spell awaits—let's create a tale that generations of magical entrepreneurs will speak of in hushed tones. Are you ready to craft your entrepreneurial legacy?

Onward we go!

Just like planting a magical seed, starting a business begins with a tiny idea. In the early stages, focus on nurturing your business seed by offering a unique product or service. Consider the needs of your customers and let your creativity blossom. This is the foundation upon which your entrepreneurial adventure will grow.

Successful entrepreneurs are like wizards who cast planning spells. Create a magical business plan—a roadmap that guides your journey, outlining your goals, target audience, and strategies for growth. This spell not only keeps you on course but also attracts potential supporters, investors, and customers to join your magical quest.

As your business takes flight, think about expanding your magical inventory. Introduce new products, services, or magical features that align with the needs and desires of your growing customer base. This ongoing expansion keeps your business vibrant and ensures it remains a beacon in the entrepreneurial landscape.

No wizard embarks on a quest alone, and neither should an entrepreneur. Cast spells of networking to connect with other business wizards, mentors, and potential partners. Collaborative ventures and partnerships can amplify the magical energy of your business, leading to shared successes and the discovery of new realms.

In today's enchanted world, the digital realm is a powerful ally for budding entrepreneurs. Learn the art of digital enchantment—utilize social media spells, create an online presence, and connect with your audience through the magic of technology. This not only broadens your reach but also strengthens the bonds with your magical community.

Just as wizards manage their magical resources, entrepreneurs practice financial alchemy. Master the art of budgeting to wisely allocate your funds and cast investment spells strategically. Whether it's expanding your product line, improving your magical storefront, or investing in marketing, make financial decisions that enhance the enchantment of your business.

Every entrepreneur's journey is a learning spell in progress. Embrace the twists, turns, and challenges as opportunities for growth. Continuously seek knowledge, learn from experiences, and adapt your strategies. This ongoing learning spell is the key to staying resilient and evolving as a magical entrepreneur.

As you stand on the brink of expanding your magical business, let's delve into the next steps to amplify the enchantment and ensure your venture stands the test of time.

Sustaining the magic of your business requires a blend of strategy, resilience, and a touch of entrepreneurial wizardry. Begin by fortifying the foundations you've laid. Ensure your products or services consistently deliver the magical experience your customers have come to expect. A satisfied customer is a loyal ally in your entrepreneurial quest.

Cast spells of customer enchantment to foster a strong connection. Listen to their feedback, respond to their needs, and continually seek ways to enhance their magical journey with your business. Happy customers not only return for more but also become ambassadors, spreading the enchantment far and wide.

In the dynamic realm of entrepreneurship, change is constant. Adaptability is your cloak of protection. Keep an eye on the winds of change in your industry, and be ready to adjust your sails. Embrace new magical trends, technologies, and customer preferences as opportunities for growth rather than challenges.

Become a master of magical metrics—tracking and analyzing key indicators of your business's health and performance. Monitor your sales spells, customer engagement potions, and financial incantations. These magical metrics unveil patterns and insights, guiding you in refining your strategies and making informed decisions.

Just as Hogwarts had its fellowship of wizards, your business needs a team of magical allies. Recruit and nurture a team that shares your vision and brings diverse magical talents to the table. A united fellowship works together to overcome challenges and celebrates the victories, making your entrepreneurial journey all the more magical.

Guard your magical realm by casting legal and ethical spells. Familiarize yourself with the laws and regulations governing your business. Ensure your magical practices align with ethical standards. This not only protects your business but also enhances its reputation, establishing it as a beacon of trust in the enchanted marketplace.

So go ahead and create your own kingdom…

8

DECISION-MAKING SKILLS: EVALUATING FINANCIAL CHOICES

Welcome to a chapter specially brewed for the wizards-in-training—"Fun Finances: The Magical Art of Money for Kids." Now, you might be wondering, "Why should we bother with money stuff? Isn't it all about spells and adventures?" Well, gather 'round, because we're about to uncover the magical secrets of why learning about money is the key to unlocking your grandest quests!

Imagine you're on a treasure hunt, seeking magical coins and enchanted gems hidden in the corners of your world. Learning about money is like having a treasure map—it guides you to where the sparkling treasures are and helps you avoid getting lost in the enchanted forest of financial mysteries.

Here's the real magic—understanding money gives you the power to make your dreams come true. Want to embark on epic adventures, create your enchanted castle, or even ride a dragon through the clouds? Money, when managed wisely, becomes your very own magic wand, turning your dreams into reality.

Every young wizard needs to master their magical choices. Learning about money is like discovering the spells that guide you in making smart choices with your coins. From buying your favorite magical treats to saving up for that special wand, your choices shape the adventure of your wizarding life.

Guess what? Learning about money can be as fun as casting spells! From playing magical money games to turning your budget into a wizardly quest, you'll discover that money isn't just about numbers—it's about crafting your own magical story.

So let's begin, shall we?

Picture this chapter as a quest—your quest to become a wise financial wizard who can make choices that sparkle with smartness and shine with magical goodness.

Imagine you're a potion-maker in the world of finance. Each decision you make is like mixing a magical potion, and your ingredients are the choices you have. Some choices are like glittery gems, while others might be a bit tricky. But fear not! With the right skills, you can craft the perfect potion for your magical financial journey.

To be a wise potion-maker, you must first understand the difference between wants and needs. Wants are like the extra toppings on your magical ice cream—they're nice to have but not necessary. Needs, on the other hand, are like the essential ingredients for your magic spells—things you can't do without.

Think of your budget as a magical map that guides you on your financial quest. With your map in hand, you can see where your money is going and plan your potion-making wisely. A good potion-maker knows how to allocate their ingredients (money) to make sure they have everything they need for a successful spell.

Now, let's talk about choosing wisely. When faced with different potions (financial choices), use your wizardly powers to evaluate them. Ask yourself, "Does this potion help me reach my magical goals? Is it a wise use of my ingredients?" Remember, not every potion is meant for every wizard, so choose the ones that align with your magical journey.

Wise wizards always think ahead. Picture a magical time-turner—a spell that helps you see into the future. Before you mix your potion, ask yourself, "Will this choice bring magic to my future self, or will it make my journey more challenging?" Thinking ahead ensures your financial potions stand the test of time.

Even the greatest wizards seek advice. Don't hesitate to ask potion masters (trusted adults or mentors) for guidance. They've been on their own financial quests and can share their wisdom to help you make the best choices.

Now that we've delved into the basics of financial decision-making, it's time to explore more magical secrets to enhance your potion-making skills. Ready to add a dash of wisdom and a sprinkle of enchantment to your financial journey? Let's dive in!

Imagine a magical potion that lets you compare different choices side by side. This potion is called the "Comparison Elixir." Before brewing any financial potion, take a sip of this elixir. It helps you see the pros and cons of each choice, ensuring you pick the one that sparkles the most.

In the magical world of finance, there's a spell called "Impulsive Temptation," and it can be quite tricky. Imagine you're at the magical market, and you see something shiny. Before casting the impulsive spell, take a moment to think. Ask yourself, "Is this a want or a need? Will it bring long-lasting magic to my journey?"

Every wise wizard knows the importance of an emergency enchantment. Life is full of surprises, and having a safety net is like having a magical shield. Consider creating a potion for emergencies—a savings spell that ensures you're prepared for unexpected twists in your financial quest.

Now, let's talk about the Growth Elixir—a potion that helps your magical coins multiply over time. Investing is like planting seeds that grow into enchanted trees of wealth. Seek advice from wise wizards (financial advisors) on how to wisely use the Growth Elixir to enhance your financial forest.

Debt can be like a dark cloud in your magical sky. But fear not! There's a spell called the "Debt Disappearing Spell." If you find yourself tangled in the web of debt, create a potion to tackle it head-on. Plan wisely, pay off high-interest debts first, and watch as your financial sky clears.

Every potion-maker deserves a celebration, and so do you! When you achieve a financial goal, whether big or small, celebrate your magical victories. It could be a small party, a special treat, or simply a dance under the stars. Celebrations infuse your financial journey with joy and motivation.

As we conclude this chapter, remember that your financial journey is an ongoing quest. Every choice you make contributes to your wizardly legacy. Keep learning, and adapting, and let the enchantment of wise decision-making shape the magical tales told about you in the realms of finance.

9

INVESTING FOR GROWTH: STOCKS, BONDS, AND MUTUAL FUNDS

Just like a wizard mastering advanced spells, you are about to embark on a journey where your financial acumen transforms your dreams into tangible treasures.

Imagine your money as mystical ingredients awaiting the touch of a skilled alchemist. Investing is the alchemy that transforms these coins into potent potions, with the power to shape your financial destiny. In this chapter, we'll unravel the mysteries of stocks, bonds, and mutual funds—the magical tools that can add wings to your financial aspirations.

Visualize stocks as your personal invitation to participate in the adventures of your favorite wizarding companies. Owning a share is like having a piece of the magic. Learn to navigate the ups and downs of stocks, for they are like the thrilling twists and turns in a captivating spell.

Enter the world of bonds, where magical agreements are made between you and other financial wizards. Bonds offer stability and a regular flow of magical interest, akin to the sweet melody of a cherished spell. Discover the art of balancing your financial symphony with these steady companions.

Mutual funds are your fellowship of financial wizards, pooling resources to achieve common goals. A wise financial wizard manages this magical alliance, guiding your coins on a collaborative journey of growth and prosperity. Learn how to join forces with fellow investors for a shared magical experience.

Picture diversification as a protective enchantment for your financial kingdom. Just as a wizard equips themselves with a variety of spells, spreading your coins across different investments shields you from the uncertainties of financial spells. Discover the art of crafting a resilient and thriving magical portfolio.

In the enchanted world of investing, time is a spell-casting companion. The Time-Traveler Spell emphasizes patience and consistency—allowing your magical coins the time they need to grow and flourish. Uncover the secrets of this powerful spell for a truly enchanting financial journey.

In this chapter, we'll embark on a thrilling quest to discover the secrets of stocks, bonds, and mutual funds—the magical tools that can turn your financial dreams into reality.

Imagine your money as seeds, waiting to be planted in the fertile soil of the financial world. Investing is the spell that transforms those seeds into flourishing gardens of wealth. Whether you dream of owning a dragon sanctuary, building a wizarding school, or simply riding on clouds, investing can help turn those dreams into reality.

Picture stocks as magical shares in your favorite wizarding companies. When you own a share, you become a part-owner of that company. It's like having a piece of the magical castle! As the company grows, so does the value of your shares. But beware, stocks can be a bit like magical creatures—they can go up and down. Learning to understand and choose the right ones is your key to success.

Now, think of bonds as magical agreements between you and other wizards, often governments or companies. When you buy a bond, it's like you're lending your coins in exchange for regular magical interest payments. Bonds are generally more stable than stocks, making them a reliable option for those who prefer a calmer financial journey.

Mutual funds are like a gathering of wizards joining forces to achieve a common goal. When you invest in a mutual fund, your coins join a pool with other wizards' coins. A professional wizard (fund manager) uses their expertise to choose a mix of stocks, bonds, and other magical assets. It's a team effort to make your coins grow.

In the world of investing, diversity is your magical shield. Just like having a variety of spells makes you a more powerful wizard, spreading your coins across different investments helps protect you from the ups and downs of the financial spells. It's the secret to creating a resilient and prosperous magical kingdom.

Here's the most powerful spell of all—patience. Investing is a long-term game, much like mastering advanced spells. The longer you let your coins grow, the more magical they become. Time is your ally, so start early, be patient, and watch the enchantment unfold.

Crafting your magical portfolio is like selecting spells for your spellbook. Consider your goals, risk tolerance, and the kind of adventures you dream of. Whether you prefer the excitement of stocks or the steady journey of bonds, building a well-balanced portfolio ensures a magical mix that aligns with your financial quest.

Now that we've dipped our toes into the magical waters of stocks, bonds, and mutual funds, let's deepen our understanding and uncover more secrets to make your investment journey even more enchanting.

Imagine you have a magical crystal ball that shows you the health and progress of your investments. This crystal ball is akin to monitoring your investment portfolio. Keep a watchful eye on how your magical coins are performing. Regularly check-in, just like you would inspect your magical tools before heading on a grand adventure.

In the wizarding world of investing, maintaining balance is crucial. Think of your portfolio as a magical seesaw. Sometimes, the value of certain investments may grow faster than others, creating an imbalance. To keep things harmonious, cast the rebalancing spell. This involves adjusting your portfolio to ensure it aligns with your original magical plan.

Even the wisest wizards seek counsel from experienced sages. In the realm of investing, these sages are financial advisors. They possess a wealth of knowledge about the magical world of finance and can provide guidance tailored to your unique journey. Seeking advice from these financial wizards ensures you're making well-informed decisions.

Imagine receiving magical potions regularly, just for being a shareholder. That's the essence of dividends! When you invest in certain stocks, companies may share their magical profits with you in the form of dividends. It's like savoring the sweet fruits of your investment garden. Reinvesting these dividends can further amplify your magical wealth.

In the magical world of investing, storms may brew—market downturns, economic shifts, or unexpected twists. Being a resilient wizard involves staying calm and weathering these storms. Keep a sturdy financial cloak, diversify your investments, and remember that, like all storms, these too shall pass.

A wise wizard is always hungry for knowledge. Explore educational portals, attend financial workshops, and read magical scrolls about investing. The more you understand the intricacies of the financial spells, the more confidently you can navigate the enchanted realms of investment.

10

FINANCIAL MATH: PRACTICAL APPLICATIONS AND REAL-LIFE SCENARIOS

In this chapter, we'll delve into the world of financial mathematics, exploring its practical applications and real-life scenarios. Financial math is the toolset that enables us to make informed decisions about money, investments, and overall financial well-being. Without further ado, let's demystify the complexities and uncover the essential aspects of financial math.

Financial math begins with the fundamentals. At its core, it involves arithmetic, percentages, and basic algebra. These foundational concepts are the building blocks for more advanced financial calculations. Mastering these basics equips you with the skills to navigate various financial scenarios.

Creating and managing a budget is a fundamental application of financial math. It involves calculating income, expenses, and allocating funds for different purposes. By employing mathematical principles, individuals and businesses can gain a clear understanding of their financial standing and make strategic decisions to achieve their financial goals.

Understanding interest is pivotal in financial math. Whether it's earning interest on savings or paying interest on loans, the concept of the time value of money comes into play. Financial math allows us to calculate compound interest, helping individuals and businesses make informed decisions regarding investments and borrowing.

Financial math is indispensable in the realm of investments. Calculating returns, assessing risks, and understanding investment performance require advanced mathematical tools. Concepts such as portfolio diversification, standard deviation, and the Sharpe ratio are employed to make strategic investment decisions based on quantitative analysis.

When it comes to real estate, financial math plays a crucial role in understanding mortgages and loan amortization. Individuals use mathematical formulas to determine monthly mortgage payments, analyze different loan options, and assess the long-term financial implications of real estate investments.

Planning for retirement involves projecting future values and understanding annuities. Financial math helps individuals estimate the amount needed for a comfortable retirement, considering factors such as inflation, expected returns, and the time horizon until retirement.

Financial math is instrumental in tax planning. Calculating taxable income, understanding deductions, and evaluating the impact of tax credits require mathematical precision. This knowledge aids individuals and businesses in optimizing their tax positions within the legal framework.

In today's data-driven world, financial math plays a crucial role in data analysis and financial modeling. From assessing market trends to predicting future financial scenarios, mathematical models provide valuable insights for making informed decisions.

Understanding the details of these applications will empower you to wield financial math as a precise and practical tool in your financial toolkit.

Budgeting Mastery:

In the realm of personal and business finance, budgeting is the cornerstone of sound financial management. Financial math comes into play as you calculate income, factor in recurring expenses, and allocate funds strategically. By employing budgeting formulas, you gain insights into your financial habits and make informed decisions to achieve financial goals.

If your monthly income is $4,000, and you allocate 30% to housing, 20% to transportation, 15% to groceries, and so on, financial math helps you create a detailed budget that aligns with your priorities.

Interest and Loans:

Interest is a powerful force in financial transactions. Financial math helps you understand how interest accrues over time, whether it's earning interest on savings or paying interest on loans. Calculating compound interest allows you to evaluate the impact of interest rates and time on the growth or cost of your financial endeavors.

If you invest $1,000 at an annual interest rate of 5%, compounded quarterly, financial math enables you to calculate the future value of your investment over different time periods.

Investment Calculations:

Investing involves calculated risks and potential returns. Financial math equips you with tools to assess investment performance and manage risk. Concepts such as standard deviation help quantify the variability of returns, enabling you to make informed decisions about portfolio diversification and risk tolerance.

Using historical data, financial math allows you to calculate the standard deviation of an investment portfolio, helping you gauge its level of risk.

Mortgages and Loan Amortization:

When venturing into real estate, financial math is indispensable for understanding mortgages and loan amortization. Calculating monthly mortgage payments, assessing the impact of interest rates, and understanding the breakdown between principal and interest payments are vital aspects of real estate mathematics.

With a $200,000 mortgage at a 4% interest rate over 30 years, financial math facilitates the calculation of monthly payments and the distribution of principal and interest over the loan term.

Retirement Planning:

Retirement planning involves projecting future values and understanding annuities. Financial math helps you estimate the amount needed for retirement by factoring in variables like expected returns, inflation, and the number of years until retirement.

Calculating the future value of regular contributions to a retirement account helps you determine the potential size of your nest egg upon retirement.

Tax Planning:

Tax planning requires precision, and financial math helps you navigate the complexities of the tax landscape. Calculating taxable income, understanding deductions, and evaluating the impact of tax credits enables you to optimize your tax position within legal frameworks.

Financial math aids in calculating taxable income by factoring in sources of income, eligible deductions, and tax credits.

Predictive Insights

In the era of data analytics, financial math is instrumental in data analysis and financial modeling. Statistical methods, regression analysis, and mathematical models provide insights into market trends, enabling informed decision-making.

Financial math can be applied to analyze historical stock prices, helping you identify trends and make predictions about future price movements.

In conclusion, financial math is not an abstract concept but a practical compass guiding your financial journey. By mastering these applications and scenarios, you empower yourself to navigate the complexities of personal and business finance. As you delve into the intricacies of financial math, remember that each calculation and analysis is a step toward financial literacy and success. May your financial journey be precise, informed, and filled with prosperity!

11

MONEY IN THE FAMILY: BUDGETING AND FINANCIAL RESPONSIBILITY

Managing finances within a family is a unique and rewarding journey that involves collaboration, communication, and shared responsibilities. Let's uncover the strategies and practices that make family budgeting not only effective but also a means to instill financial responsibility in each member.

Creating a family budget is akin to crafting a blueprint for financial harmony. Financial math becomes a powerful ally as you calculate income, outline expenses, and allocate funds for various needs. A family budget provides a clear roadmap, ensuring that financial resources are utilized wisely to meet the family's goals and aspirations.

By setting aside a portion of the budget for education, entertainment, and savings, families can align their financial priorities with the collective vision for the future.

In a family, everyone plays a role in the financial ecosystem. Financial responsibility is not just about managing money; it's about fostering a sense of mindfulness and accountability. Assigning age-appropriate financial responsibilities to each family member instills valuable lessons about money management and accountability.

Children might have responsibilities like saving a portion of their allowance, while adults handle larger expenses. This collaborative approach builds a sense of ownership and responsibility.

Money in the family is an excellent platform for imparting essential money values. Open and honest conversations about the family's financial situation, decision-making processes, and the importance of savings lay the foundation for a healthy financial mindset. These discussions create an environment where family members can learn from one another's experiences and perspectives.

Discussing the family's financial goals, like saving for a vacation or a future home, involves everyone in the decision-making process and instills a shared sense of purpose.

Every family encounters unexpected challenges, and having a financial safety net is crucial. Establishing an emergency fund becomes a collective effort, ensuring that the family is prepared for unforeseen circumstances. Moreover, future planning, including education funds and retirement savings, becomes a shared commitment to long-term financial security.

Allocating a portion of the family budget to an emergency fund reinforces the importance of preparedness, while contributions to education and retirement accounts demonstrate a commitment to the family's future well-being.

In the family setting, financial literacy is a gift that keeps on giving. From teaching young children the basics of money through games and activities to guiding teenagers through the intricacies of budgeting and investing, the family becomes a microcosm of financial education. Empowering each family member with financial knowledge sets the stage for a lifetime of informed decision-making.

Implementing a weekly family finance session where everyone shares their financial insights or learns a new money-related concept fosters a culture of continuous learning.

Financial achievements, both big and small, deserve to be celebrated. Whether it's reaching a savings goal, successfully adhering to the budget, or making a collective financial decision, acknowledging these milestones fosters a positive and supportive family dynamic. Celebrations reinforce the idea that financial success is a shared journey.

A family outing or a special treat can be a simple yet meaningful way to celebrate financial milestones and create positive associations with responsible money management.

Families, like finances, go through different seasons. The ability to adapt the family budget to changing circumstances and communicate openly about financial challenges is vital. Whether it's adjusting spending during challenging times or collectively planning for major expenses, adaptability, and communication are the keys to maintaining financial stability.

Communicating openly about changes in income, expenses, or financial goals allows the family to make informed decisions and navigate financial seasons together.

As we continue our exploration of "Money in the Family," let's delve into more facets of family budgeting and financial responsibility. The journey we're on involves not just managing the present but also preparing for the financial adventures that lie ahead. So, gather around as we uncover additional strategies for nurturing a financially savvy and resilient family unit.

Setting collective savings goals as a family not only reinforces financial responsibility but also creates a sense of unity. Whether it's saving for a dream vacation, a home, or a special family event, working together toward a common financial goal strengthens the familial bond while teaching the importance of planning and perseverance.

Establishing a "Family Dream Board" where everyone contributes ideas for a shared financial goal and tracks progress fosters a collaborative and goal-oriented mindset.

Each family member, regardless of age, can benefit from tailored financial education. Younger children might engage in activities that introduce basic financial concepts, while teenagers could delve into more complex topics like budgeting, investing, and credit. Customizing financial lessons ensures that everyone in the family is equipped with age-appropriate knowledge.

Implementing a "Financial Book Club" where different family members read and discuss books or articles related to their respective age groups enhances financial literacy across generations.

Introducing allowances to children offers an early lesson in financial independence. By managing their own money, children learn to make choices, budget, and experience the consequences of their financial decisions. This hands-on experience sets the stage for responsible money management in their adult lives.

Allowing children to allocate their allowance for spending, saving, and giving encourages a sense of autonomy and teaches valuable money management skills.

An environment of financial transparency within the family encourages open discussions about money matters. From family budget reviews to explaining the impact of financial decisions, transparency fosters a culture where questions are welcomed, and concerns are addressed collectively. This openness helps demystify financial concepts and cultivates a shared sense of responsibility.

Conducting regular "Family Finance Meetings" where everyone has a chance to share updates, ask questions, and discuss financial decisions promotes transparency and inclusivity.

Family financial responsibility extends beyond the household. Engaging in community-oriented financial activities, such as charitable giving or participating in local initiatives, teaches family members about social responsibility. These experiences provide valuable lessons about using financial resources to contribute positively to the community.

Participating as a family in a local charity event or collectively deciding on a cause to support financially instills a sense of social responsibility.

Life is full of financial challenges, and facing them as a family can be a transformative experience. Whether it's navigating economic downturns, unexpected expenses, or teaching the importance of an emergency fund, these challenges become opportunities to reinforce resilience and the ability to adapt to changing financial circumstances.

Creating a "Family Emergency Fund Challenge" where everyone contributes to building a fund for unexpected expenses cultivates resilience and preparedness.

In the digital age, technology and FinTech tools offer innovative ways to manage family finances. Exploring budgeting apps, setting up shared financial goals online, and utilizing digital tools for financial education add a modern dimension to family financial management. Embracing technology ensures that family members are equipped to navigate the evolving financial landscape.

Adopting a family budgeting app that allows members to track expenses, set savings goals, and monitor progress in real-time harnesses the power of technology for efficient financial management.

As we wrap up this chapter, remember that the journey of family financial responsibility is an ongoing adventure. By continuing to adapt, communicate openly, and embrace financial education, you're not just managing money—you're empowering future generations with the knowledge and skills to thrive in their financial quests.

12

CREDIT AND DEBIT: MANAGING PLASTIC CARDS WISELY

Ever thought about credit and debit cards?

These tiny pieces of plastic wield great financial power, offering convenience, flexibility, and the potential for building or damaging your financial kingdom. Let's unravel the mysteries of credit and debit cards and discover the art of managing them wisely.

Credit cards are like magical wands that grant you access to a pool of funds. However, wielding this financial power requires caution and responsibility. Credit cards allow you to make purchases on credit, with the understanding that you'll repay the borrowed amount. It's crucial to use credit cards wisely, as mishandling them can lead to high-interest debts and financial challenges.

Making a $500 purchase on a credit card and repaying the full amount by the due date allows you to enjoy the convenience of credit without incurring interest charges.

Unlike credit cards, debit cards provide direct access to your own funds. When you use a debit card, you're essentially spending money that's already in your bank account. Debit cards offer convenience without the risk of accumulating debt. However, it's essential to monitor your account balance to avoid overdrawing and incurring fees.

Using a debit card for everyday expenses ensures that you're spending within your means, as each transaction directly deducts from your available funds.

Credit cards often come with interest rates, which represent the cost of borrowing money if you carry a balance. It's crucial to understand these rates and, whenever possible, pay off the full balance each month to avoid accruing interest charges. Being mindful of interest rates helps you make informed decisions about when to use credit and when to opt for alternative payment methods.

If your credit card has an annual percentage rate (APR) of 18%, carrying a $1,000 balance for a year would result in $180 in interest charges.

Credit cards play a significant role in building your credit history, a record of your borrowing and repayment behavior. A positive credit history is crucial for future financial endeavors, such as applying for loans or mortgages. Responsible credit card use, including timely payments and maintaining low balances, contributes to a favorable credit score.

Consistently making on-time credit card payments and keeping credit card balances low positively impacts your credit score over time.

Every credit card comes with a credit limit—the maximum amount you can borrow. Exceeding this limit can result in penalties and fees. It's essential to be aware of your credit limit and use credit cards within this boundary to avoid negative consequences.

If your credit card has a $5,000 limit, keeping your balance below this threshold ensures you stay within your credit card's magical barrier.

Debit cards, directly linked to your bank account, require careful protection. Ensure that you safeguard your card details, monitor your transactions regularly, and report any unauthorized activities promptly. This diligence helps prevent fraudulent activities and ensures the security of your financial realm.

Regularly checking your bank statements and setting up alerts for unusual transactions adds an extra layer of security to your debit card usage.

Many credit cards come with reward programs and cashback incentives. These magical bonuses can add value to your financial journey when used wisely. Understanding the terms and conditions of these programs allows you to maximize the benefits without falling into the trap of overspending.

Using a credit card with a cashback program for regular expenses like groceries can result in earned cashback over time.

The journey continues, and there are more magical insights to uncover as we navigate the nuances of interest rates, responsible spending, and crafting a harmonious relationship with your cards.

Using credit cards wisely involves a delicate balancing act. While they provide convenience and financial flexibility, it's crucial to strike a balance between credit utilization and repayment. Aim to keep your credit card balances low relative to your credit limit, ensuring a healthy credit utilization ratio. Responsible credit card practices contribute to a positive credit history and score.

If your credit limit is $5,000, keeping your balance below $1,000 (20% utilization) is a smart practice for maintaining a positive credit profile.

One of the most potent spells in credit card management is paying the full balance each month. By doing so, you avoid interest charges altogether, ensuring that your magical financial powers remain untarnished. Cultivate the habit of paying your credit card bill in full and on time to harness the true potential of credit cards without falling into the interest trap.

If your credit card statement shows a balance of $1,000, paying the full $1,000 by the due date prevents the accrual of interest charges.

While credit cards offer the flexibility of making minimum payments, relying solely on this option can lead to the interest curse. Minimum payments may cover only a fraction of the total balance, resulting in the accumulation of interest over time. To break free from the interest curse, strive to pay more than the minimum whenever possible.

If your credit card statement requires a minimum payment of $25, paying $100 significantly reduces the impact of interest on your outstanding balance.

Your credit card statement is a treasure trove of information. Scrutinize it regularly to unveil hidden truths about your spending habits, fees, and any unauthorized transactions. By staying vigilant and promptly addressing discrepancies, you protect yourself from financial surprises and ensure the integrity of your magical financial realm.

Reviewing your credit card statement reveals any unfamiliar charges, allowing you to report them to the card issuer for investigation and resolution.

Credit cards often serve as a financial safety net during emergencies. However, relying solely on credit in times of need can lead to debt spells. To shield yourself against debt, prioritize building and maintaining an emergency fund. Having a fund for unexpected expenses reduces the reliance on credit and promotes financial resilience.

Establishing an emergency fund equivalent to three to six months' worth of living expenses provides a robust shield against unforeseen financial challenges.

While debit cards offer direct access to your funds, exercising caution is essential. Keep a close eye on your account balance to avoid overdrawing and incurring fees. Additionally, refrain from using debit cards for large purchases where credit cards might offer added protections. Mindful spending with debit cards ensures financial stability and responsible money management.

Checking your account balance before making a purchase ensures that you have sufficient funds and prevents overdrawing on your debit card.

Regularly monitoring your credit is a powerful shield for your credit castle. Utilize free credit reports and monitoring services to stay informed about changes to your credit history. Monitoring helps detect potential issues early on and allows you to take corrective actions to maintain a pristine credit kingdom.

Checking your credit report annually and utilizing credit monitoring apps ensures that you are promptly alerted to any suspicious activity or errors in your credit history.

As we conclude this chapter on managing credit and debit cards wisely, remember that your mastery of these plastic cards is an ongoing journey. By practicing smart credit card habits, paying attention to your statements, and cultivating a healthy relationship with your cards, you empower yourself to wield these financial tools with precision.

13

PHILANTHROPY AND SOCIAL IMPACT: MAKING A DIFFERENCE WITH MONEY

Beyond the realm of personal finance, your financial powers can be harnessed to make a positive difference in the world. Let's discover the art of giving, the impact of charitable actions, and how your money can be a force for good.

Philanthropy is the act of giving to promote the welfare of others. It's not just about money; it's about the intention behind your giving. Whether supporting a cause close to your heart or contributing to a community in need, philanthropy involves a deliberate and purposeful act of making a positive impact.

Donating to a local animal shelter because you are passionate about animal welfare is a heartfelt act of philanthropy.

To maximize your social impact, identify causes that resonate with your values and beliefs. Whether it's environmental conservation, education, healthcare, or social justice, aligning your philanthropic efforts with causes you are passionate about ensures that your contributions make a meaningful difference.

Choosing to support a literacy program because you believe in the transformative power of education reflects your philanthropic compass.

Integrating philanthropy into your financial plan involves allocating funds specifically for charitable giving. By budgeting for philanthropy, you ensure that your giving aligns with your overall financial goals and priorities. This intentional approach allows you to make a sustained impact over time.

Allocating 5% of your annual income for philanthropy in your budget ensures a consistent and impactful contribution to causes you care about.

Researching Charities:

Before contributing to a charitable organization, conduct thorough research to understand their mission, impact, and financial transparency. Reputable charities provide detailed information about how donations are used, ensuring that your money directly contributes to the intended cause.

Reviewing a charity's financial reports and impact assessments ensures that your contribution is making a transparent and positive difference.

Volunteerism:

Philanthropy extends beyond financial donations. Volunteering your time and skills is a powerful way to contribute to a cause. Whether mentoring, participating in community projects, or offering professional expertise, your hands-on involvement amplifies the impact of your philanthropic efforts.

Volunteering at a local soup kitchen not only provides direct assistance to those in need but also strengthens community bonds.

Impact Investing:

Consider exploring impact investing, where your financial resources are directed toward businesses or projects that generate positive social and environmental outcomes. Impact investing allows you to align your financial goals with your values, creating a dual benefit of financial returns and societal impact.

Investing in a renewable energy project that addresses environmental concerns while generating financial returns exemplifies impact investing.

Legacy Planning:

Incorporate philanthropy into your legacy planning to perpetuate your positive impact beyond your lifetime. Establishing charitable trusts, endowments, or including charitable bequests in your will ensures that your financial legacy continues to make a difference for generations to come.

Creating a scholarship fund in your will to support underprivileged students perpetuates your commitment to education even after you are gone.

Corporate Social Responsibility (CSR):

If you are a business owner or part of a corporation, consider incorporating corporate social responsibility into your company's mission. CSR initiatives not only contribute to societal well-being but also enhance your company's reputation and employee morale.

Implementing eco-friendly practices in your business operations or supporting community development projects as part of your company's CSR demonstrates a commitment to social impact.

Educating Others:

Part of your philanthropic journey involves inspiring others to join the cause. Whether through discussions, workshops, or social media, share your experiences and knowledge to cultivate a culture of giving. Educating others amplifies the collective impact of philanthropy.

Hosting a workshop on philanthropy in your community encourages others to discover the joy and fulfillment of giving back.

Now that we've explored the magical world of helping others, let's dive deeper into the adventures of making a difference with our money. Being a hero doesn't always mean wearing capes; sometimes, it means using our magic coins to create smiles and spread joy. Join us on this exciting journey, and let's discover how even the smallest acts of kindness can have the biggest impact!

Just like picking your favorite ice cream flavor, smart giving means choosing causes that make your heart happy. Whether it's helping animals, making sure everyone has enough to eat, or supporting kids who need school supplies, your magical donations can bring joy to others and make the world a better place.

Imagine donating your birthday money to a local animal shelter to help furry friends find loving homes. That's smart giving with a sprinkle of kindness!

Teamwork Makes the Dream Work:

Remember when you and your friends teamed up to build an epic LEGO castle? Philanthropy is a bit like that—it's even more powerful when we work together! Grab your friends, classmates, or family members, and combine your magical coins to make an even bigger impact on the causes you care about.

Organize a school fundraiser with your friends to collect money for new books in your school library. Teamwork makes the dream of a fantastic library come true!

Counting Kindness:

Just like keeping score in your favorite game, you can count the kindness you spread with your magical money. Create a kindness journal or a colorful chart to track how much good you've done. Each time you help someone or donate to a cause, add a sparkle to your chart. It's a magical way to see the positive impact you're making!

Every time you help a friend or donate some of your allowance to a good cause, mark it on your kindness chart. Watch the kindness grow like a garden of magical flowers!

Little Acts, Big Smiles:

You don't need a magic wand to make the world brighter—a sprinkle of kindness works just as well! Little acts, like sharing toys, helping a friend with homework, or planting flowers in your neighborhood, can create big smiles. Your magical actions can inspire others to spread kindness too...

Surprise your neighbor with a handmade card or offer to help them carry groceries. Your small act of kindness will make their day shine!

The Magic of Sharing:

Have you ever noticed that when you share your toys or snacks, the fun multiplies? The same magic happens with money! When you share even a little bit of your magical coins with others in need, it creates a ripple of happiness. Sharing is like making a wish for joy and watching it come true!

If you have extra toys or clothes that you don't use, consider donating them to children who might not have as much. It's like sharing the magic of play and laughter!

Learning with Kindness:

Imagine going to school and not having the books, pencils, and backpacks you need to learn and have fun. With your magical money, you can help kids just like you around the world get the tools they need for a fantastic education. Your kindness becomes a magical book that opens doors to a world of learning!

Save a portion of your allowance to donate to organizations that provide school supplies to kids in different parts of the world. Your kindness helps others learn and grow!

Growing a Forest of Good Deeds:

Have you ever planted seeds in the garden and watched them grow into beautiful flowers? Well, every act of kindness is like planting a magical seed that grows into something wonderful. By spreading kindness with your money, you're growing a forest of good deeds that will make the world a more enchanted place!

Save a little bit of your magical money each month to donate to a tree-planting organization. Your kindness helps the earth grow greener and healthier!

Just like passing on your favorite storybook to a friend, you can pass on the magic of kindness! Share your favorite ways to help others with your friends and encourage them to join the adventure. The more friends with kindness wands, the more magic we can create together!

Tell your friends about the fun ways you're helping others and invite them to join in. Together, you'll create a magical circle of kindness that keeps growing!

14

CREATIVE SAVING TECHNIQUES: INVESTMENT AND FINANCIAL GOALS

Get ready for an exciting adventure as we dive into the magical world of saving money in creative and fun ways. Just like wizards have spellbooks, we have special techniques to grow our money and achieve our financial goals. Let's discover how saving and investing can be as fun as a treasure hunt!

Imagine having a magical jar where you collect coins and watch them multiply like magic! The enchanted jar spell is all about saving your coins in a special place, like a piggy bank or a colorful jar. Every time you add a coin, you're one step closer to your magical goals—whether it's a new toy, a cool gadget, or a fun adventure.

Decorate your savings jar with stickers, draw your magical goals on it, and watch your coins turn into treasures…

Wizards have wish lists for the magical items they want, and you can have a wish list too! Create a scroll (or a list) of the things you want to save money for. It could be a new game, a special outing, or even a gift for someone you care about. Your wish list will guide your saving adventures and make them even more exciting.

Draw or write your wishes on a colorful scroll and hang it up where you can see it every day. It's like casting a spell to make your wishes come true!

Every adventurer needs a treasure map, and you're no different! Create a treasure map to guide you on your saving quest. Mark the spots where you'll save money, like finding coins under your pillow or saving a portion of your allowance. As you follow your map, you'll see your money grow and get closer to discovering the treasure!

Draw a map with colorful paths and mark the spots where you'll save money. Each path leads you to a treasure—your financial goals!

Just like a wizard's time-turner, your coins can work magic over time! Understand the power of patience and watch your money grow by saving consistently. Each coin you save is like a magical tick on the clock, bringing you closer to your goals. The more time you give your coins, the more magical they become…

Choose a special day each week to add coins to your enchanted jar. Over time, you'll see how your small contributions turn into a magical treasure.

Now, let's add a touch of investment magic to your savings! Imagine your money growing faster by using a magical spell called "investing." Investing means letting your money work for you, like planting seeds that grow into enchanted trees. Learn about simple investments, like a savings account or a piggy bank that pays you extra coins for keeping your money there.

Ask your family about setting up a savings account or use a special piggy bank that adds a little extra to your savings each month. Your money will grow like magic!

Just like wizards learn new spells, you can discover ways to earn extra coins! Create your own potion of earning spells by exploring small tasks or chores that you can do to earn money. Maybe you can help with household chores, assist a neighbor, or even start a small business like selling homemade crafts. Your earning spells will add extra magic to your saving adventures!

Offer to help with tasks around the house or set up a small lemonade stand to earn extra coins for your enchanted jar. It's like mixing a potion of earning spells!

True wizards use their magic to help others, and you can too! Create a giving back charm by setting aside a portion of your savings for charity or to surprise someone special. Your giving back charm adds a heartwarming touch to your saving adventures, making them even more magical.

Choose a cause you care about, like helping animals or supporting a local charity. Set aside a portion of your savings to create a giving back charm and spread kindness!

Now that you've unleashed the magic of saving and set sail on your financial adventures, let's dive deeper into the enchanted realm of creative saving. Grab your wizard hats, and let's explore how your coins can transform into treasures through the power of planning, investing, and discovering new ways to earn magical coins.

Just like a treasure map guides a pirate to hidden gems, your wish list scroll is your magical blueprint. It's a roadmap that unveils the treasures you aim to uncover by saving your magical coins. This scroll isn't just a list; it's your guide, your companion on the journey to financial success. As you cast your gaze upon it, let the excitement of achieving your goals fuel your saving spell.

Your saving quest is a grand adventure, and every adventurer needs a map. Picture your treasure map leading you through a mystical forest of financial goals. As you follow the winding paths, marked by your saving spots, you'll discover the hidden treasures awaiting you. Embrace the thrill of the journey, for every step brings you closer to unlocking the magical chest of your dreams.

Patience is the greatest spell in your wizard's arsenal. Like a time-turning coin, it has the power to transform the ordinary into the extraordinary. As you drop your coins into the enchanted jar week after week, watch how the magic of time turns them into a dazzling collection of financial wonders. Your coins may seem small today, but with patience, they will blossom into a mighty treasure.

Let's unlock the door to a secret chamber of financial enchantment—the investment spell. Picture your coins as seeds planted in a magical garden. By choosing wise investments, you allow your money to sprout and grow into a flourishing forest of wealth. Seek the guidance of the financial wizards around you to ensure your coins multiply like magic.

Every wizard brews their unique potions, and so can you! Your potion of earning spells is a concoction of creativity, resourcefulness, and a dash of entrepreneurial spirit. Consider small tasks or ventures that align with your abilities, and watch as your potion transforms into a stream of magical coins. Earning spells not only add flair to your adventures but open new avenues for financial empowerment.

In the wizarding world, true magic lies in spreading kindness. As you embark on your financial adventures, weave a giving back charm into the fabric of your saving journey. Set aside a portion of your treasures to support causes dear to your heart or surprise someone in need. The giving back charm turns your financial quests into a force for good, making your magic resonate far beyond your enchanted jar.

15

YOUNG INVESTORS: EXPLORING THE WORLD OF STOCKS

Get ready to discover the secrets of the stock market, where dreams can turn into reality and where the adventures of young investors unfold. Let the journey begin!

Imagine a realm where tiny pieces of companies, called stocks, come to life and dance on the stage of the stock market. The stock market is like a grand wizarding marketplace where investors buy and sell these magical pieces. Each stock you own is a ticket to becoming a part-owner of a real company, and the stock market is the magical arena where these ownership spells are cast.

Just like a wizard studies their spellbook, young investors must understand the wizard's scroll of stock ownership. When you buy a stock, you're not just collecting a piece of paper; you're claiming a stake in a company's magic. The more stocks you own, the more say you have in the company's enchanted decisions. Unravel the wizard's scroll to uncover the secrets of being a true stockholder.

Now, it's time to cast your investing spell! Buying stocks is like adding magical ingredients to your potion, and selling is like choosing when to reveal your potion's power. With the guidance of your financial mentors, you'll learn the art of casting spells wisely. Whether you're seeking long-term enchantments or stirring up short-term magic, the stock market is your spellbound playground.

Every wizard needs a crystal ball, and for young investors, it's the crystal ball of research. Dive into the magical realms of financial statements, company histories, and market trends. Peering into this crystal ball helps you understand a company's past, present, and potential future. The more you gaze, the clearer your vision becomes, guiding your stock-picking spells.

Just as flying on a broomstick brings both excitement and risks, investing in stocks is a magical journey of risks and rewards. Understand that the stock market's enchantment can sometimes be unpredictable. While your investments may soar like magical creatures, they can also face storms. Equip yourself with knowledge and a steady broomstick to navigate the ups and downs of the investing sky.

Wise wizards know the importance of a balanced potion, and young investors, too, should craft a balanced portfolio. The potion of diversification involves spreading your magical ingredients (investments) across different stocks. By diversifying, you reduce the impact of any single potion gone awry, ensuring your financial cauldron stays steady and strong.

In the stock market, dividends are like golden elixirs bestowed upon faithful wizards. When you own stocks, some companies share their magical profits with you through dividends. These golden elixirs can be reinvested to grow your stock portfolio or collected to fuel your own magical adventures. Embrace our exploration of the enchanting world of stocks as we delve deeper into the magical practices that define young investors. Grab your metaphorical wands, for there's more to unravel in the realm of financial wizardry. Let's journey further into the secrets of the stock market and uncover the additional layers of its magical tapestry.

Just as wizards have familiar creatures by their side, young investors have market indices as their guardians. These magical creatures represent groups of stocks that share common characteristics. Understanding market index magic helps you gauge the overall health and performance of the enchanted market. Keep an eye on these familiars to gain insights into the broader magical landscape.

In the wizarding world, time-turners allow for extraordinary temporal adventures. Similarly, long-term investing is your time-turner strategy in the stock market. Embrace the magic of patience and watch your investments unfold over the years. With the power of compounding, your financial spells become more potent, turning small investments into substantial treasures.

Just as the phoenix rises from its ashes, young investors can navigate market volatility and emerge stronger. The stock market, like the magical phoenix, experiences ups and downs. Instead of fearing volatility, embrace it as an opportunity. During market downturns, consider it a chance to purchase magical ingredients (stocks) at discounted prices, preparing for the inevitable rise.

Even the most skilled sorcerers make mistakes, and young investors are no different. View your financial journey as the apprenticeship of a sorcerer, where learning from mistakes becomes a powerful spell. Every misstep is a chance to refine your magical techniques and become a more adept financial wizard. Embrace the lessons, for they are steppingstones to mastering the art of investing.

Behind every successful wizard is a potion of patience and discipline. Mastering your financial spells involves cultivating these essential qualities. Stay patient during market fluctuations, and discipline yourself to stick to your investing strategy. The potion of patience and discipline ensures that your magical journey remains focused, steady, and aligned with your long-term goals.

No sorcerer walks the magical path alone, and neither should young investors. Seek the counsel of the Council of Financial Wizards—experienced mentors, teachers, or family members who possess financial wisdom. Learning from their magical insights can enhance your understanding of the stock market and provide valuable guidance on your financial odyssey. the joy of earning dividends, and watching your financial spells flourish.

Embark on the quest for long-term growth, where patience becomes your most potent magical ally. Just as wizards grow wiser with time, long-term investing allows your stocks to mature and flourish. Set your sights on distant horizons, and let the magic of compounding transform your humble investments into a majestic castle of wealth.

As we approach the grand finale of this chapter, remember that your journey as a young investor is an ongoing saga. Unleash the power of ownership spells, cast your investing spells wisely, and let the crystal ball of research illuminate your path. Embrace the magical creatures of market indices, wield the time-turner strategy, and rise like the phoenix through market volatility. Learn from your sorcerer's apprenticeship, brew the potion of patience and discipline, and seek the guidance of the Council of Financial Wizards.

16

REAL-WORLD MONEY CHALLENGES: PROBLEM-SOLVING SKILLS

It's time to put your financial knowledge to the test and hone your problem-solving skills. Join us on a journey where the magic lies in applying what you've learned to conquer real-world financial challenges. Let's embark on this practical adventure together!

Your first challenge on the real-world money quest is to craft the budget spell. Imagine your budget as a powerful incantation that helps you control and direct your money. Break down your income, allocate funds for needs and wants, and watch how your budget spell transforms your financial landscape. The budget spell is your key to financial independence, guiding you through the labyrinth of income and expenses.

Alchemy isn't just a magical concept—it's a real-world skill, and your coins are the magical ingredients. Turn your coins into gold through the alchemy of saving. As middle and high schoolers, you have the power to save for short-term goals like a new gadget or long-term dreams like higher education. Master the art of saving, and witness how your financial potions evolve into golden treasures.

Taxes might seem like a mysterious potion, but they're a part of the real-world financial landscape. Your challenge is to become a tax wizard, understanding the basics of income tax, deductions, and credits. Learn to decode the tax enigma, ensuring that your financial spells comply with the rules of the financial kingdom. Being a tax wizard empowers you to keep more of your magical earnings.

Credit is like a protective shield in the financial realm, and your challenge is to enchant it wisely. Explore the concept of credit, understand its power, and learn how to build a strong financial shield through responsible credit practices. Whether it's obtaining a credit card or taking out a loan, the credit enchantment safeguards your financial future.

The time has come to unleash the magic of investments in the real world. Dive into the realms of stocks, bonds, and mutual funds, wielding the power of your financial knowledge. As middle and high schoolers, you can start small with investments and watch them grow into mighty financial forces. The real-world challenge is to navigate the investment landscape and witness your wealth flourish.

Your journey into the real world includes crafting your career spell through the enchanted job search. Learn the art of resume crafting, interview spells, and networking enchantments. Your goal is to secure internships, part-time jobs, or explore career paths aligned with your aspirations. The enchanted job search is your gateway to earning and learning in the real-world arena.

Life is an unpredictable adventure, and your challenge is to shield against its surprises through the insurance chronicles. Understand the magic of insurance—from health to auto to renter's insurance. The insurance chronicles equip you with financial armor, ensuring that unexpected twists in your life's journey don't disrupt your financial equilibrium.

True wizards use their magic to benefit others, and as high schoolers, you're ready for the charity quest. Explore ways to spread your financial goodwill, whether it's through volunteering, supporting local causes, or contributing to charitable organizations. The charity quest amplifies the impact of your financial magic, creating positive ripples in the real-world community.

As you conquer real-world money challenges, take time for a financial reflection. Evaluate your journey, celebrate your successes, and learn from any missteps. The financial reflection is your enchanted mirror, reflecting the growth of your problem-solving skills and the evolution of your financial wizardry.

Brace yourselves for the next set of challenges, each designed to test your financial mettle and cultivate the wizard within.

For many high schoolers, the education maze leads to a student loan conundrum. Your challenge is to navigate this maze wisely, understanding the terms and implications of student loans. Explore options for scholarships, grants, and part-time work to support your education. The student loan conundrum is a gateway to knowledge, and your financial wisdom will be your guiding light.

As you embark on your journey into the real world, the wheels of fortune await you in the form of the automobile spell. Decoding this spell involves understanding the true cost of owning a car—from purchasing to maintenance and insurance. As middle and high schoolers, you're at the crossroads of gaining independence, and the automobile spell challenges you to make informed decisions regarding transportation.

As you step into adulthood, the housing havens beckon. Whether it's renting your first apartment or leasing a shared space, the challenge lies in understanding the contractual spells involved. Dive into the art of renting and leasing, exploring your rights and responsibilities as a tenant. Housing havens are a cornerstone of independence, and mastering this spell ensures a secure and comfortable abode.

For those with entrepreneurial ambitions, crafting your business incantation is the next challenge. Explore the realm of small business ownership, from ideation to execution. Understand the financial spells required to launch and sustain a venture. The entrepreneurial spell empowers you to turn your passions into profitable pursuits, fostering financial independence and creativity.

As you engage in the marketplace alchemy, the art of negotiation takes center stage. Hone your skills in striking fair deals, whether it's salary negotiations, purchasing goods, or securing services. The marketplace alchemy challenges you to harness the power of persuasion and diplomacy in your real-world transactions.

While retirement may seem distant, casting the long-term security spell is a challenge worth undertaking. Explore retirement savings options, such as employer-sponsored plans or individual retirement accounts (IRAs). The retirement enigma is your opportunity to secure a future where financial independence and relaxation coexist.

In the unpredictable realm of life, financial emergencies may arise. Your challenge is to craft the resilience elixir, preparing for unexpected events. Establish an emergency fund to shield against unforeseen expenses and challenges. The resilience elixir ensures that you navigate life's twists and turns with financial fortitude.

As you advance in your financial journey, the legacy spell beckons. Explore ways to create a lasting financial impact, whether through investments, philanthropy, or wise financial teachings. The legacy spell challenges you to think beyond the present, considering the mark you wish to leave on the financial world.

No wizard conquers challenges alone, and the financial fellowship is your key to building a supportive network. Connect with mentors, advisors, and peers who can provide guidance and share their experiences. The financial fellowship enriches your journey, offering insights and camaraderie as you navigate the real-world financial landscape.

As we approach the conclusion of this chapter on real-world money challenges, remember that your financial saga is a dynamic, ever-evolving narrative. Tackle the student loan conundrum, decipher the automobile spell, navigate housing havens, embark on entrepreneurial pursuits, master the art of negotiation, cast the long-term security spell, craft the resilience elixir, explore the legacy spell, and build a robust financial fellowship. Your real-world financial saga is a canvas waiting for the strokes of your financial wand.

17

EXPLORING FINANCIAL CAREERS: DREAM JOBS IN FINANCE

Forget the jargon; we're going to explore cool jobs that help make money work like magic. Let's find out how you can turn your dreams into reality in the financial world and maybe even discover your dream job!

Imagine being a money mover, helping people keep their money safe and accessible. Bankers and tellers are like financial superheroes who assist you with savings, withdrawals, and even guide you on making smart money moves. They make sure your money is in the right place at the right time.

If you enjoy playing with numbers and making sure everything adds up perfectly, you might be a numbers wizard! Accountants and auditors help individuals and businesses manage their finances. They ensure that all the numbers are accurate, like magic math detectives who solve financial puzzles.

Financial planners are like money artists who help families and individuals create masterpieces with their finances. They listen to your dreams, understand your goals, and craft plans to make them come true. It's like having a personal guide for your money adventures!

Ever thought about being a money guardian? Insurance agents protect people from unexpected surprises by offering magical shields called insurance. They help you prepare for the unexpected twists and turns in life, making sure you're always financially secure.

Investment advisors are like money explorers who guide people on exciting journeys to grow their money. They help you understand the magic of investments, like buying pieces of companies or watching your money grow over time. It's like having a financial compass pointing you toward wealth!

Have you ever dreamed of building something amazing? Entrepreneurs are like money builders who create their own businesses. They turn their ideas into reality, providing products or services that people need. Being an entrepreneur is like having your own magical kingdom of business!

Sales professionals are fantastic negotiators who help people find what they need and want. They connect buyers and sellers, making sure everyone gets a fair deal. It's like being a financial matchmaker, bringing together people and products in a magical marketplace.

Urban planners are like city architects who plan the layout of neighborhoods and cities. They decide where buildings, parks, and roads should go to create thriving communities. It's like designing a magical cityscape where everyone can live happily ever after!

If you love telling stories and sharing information, you might be a money communicator! Journalists and writers in finance write articles, create stories, and share important financial news. They're like magical messengers, keeping everyone informed about the financial adventures happening around the world.

Security experts are like money protectors who ensure that our financial information stays safe. They use special tools and techniques to guard against bad magic—like hackers and other digital villains. Being a security expert is like having a shield that keeps everyone's money and information secure.

Our adventure into the world of finance careers continues, and there's so much more to uncover. Let's explore additional dream jobs that make money matters even more exciting. From technology wizards to community builders, each role plays a unique part in the financial story. Get ready to discover your potential dream job in the world of finance!

Imagine being a money innovator, someone who uses technology to make financial activities more fun and accessible. Fintech developers create apps and games that help you learn about money in a playful way. It's like having a magical device that makes managing money a breeze!

Financial analysts are like money conductors who study patterns and trends to help people make smart money decisions. They analyze financial data and provide insights, helping individuals and businesses orchestrate their financial strategies. It's like reading a magical map that guides you to financial success!

Graphic designers in finance are like artists who bring financial concepts to life through visuals. They create magical infographics, illustrations, and designs that make learning about money not only informative but also a feast for the eyes. It's like having a magical picture book that makes finance come alive!

Have you ever dreamed of connecting with people from all around the world? International bankers are like money ambassadors who work with global finances. They help businesses and individuals manage money across different countries, making the world feel like a magical neighborhood.

For those who love nature, being a money steward might be the perfect fit. Environmental economists focus on how money and resources impact the environment. They work towards creating a magical balance between economic activities and preserving the beauty of our planet.

Just like therapists help people navigate their feelings, financial counselors are like money therapists who assist individuals and families in managing their financial emotions. They provide guidance on budgeting, saving, and dealing with money stress. It's like having a magical advisor for your financial well-being...

Copywriters in finance are like wordsmiths who use their magical pens to create compelling stories and content about money. They craft messages that make financial topics engaging and easy to understand. It's like reading a magical storybook that makes money lessons fun.

Ever thought about being a teacher who makes money lessons exciting? Educators in finance are like money explainers who share their knowledge with students. They make learning about money a magical experience, equipping the next generation with the tools to navigate the financial world.

If you love helping families plan for their future, being a financial planner for families is a fantastic dream job. These money adventurers guide families on their financial journey, helping them achieve their goals and dreams. It's like being a co-captain on a magical family voyage!

18

FINANCIAL INDEPENDENCE: MANAGING PERSONAL FINANCES

In this chapter, we'll embark on a magical journey towards achieving financial independence by mastering the art of managing personal finances. While we won't be conjuring spells or waving wands, we'll delve into practical steps and strategies that will empower you to take control of your money. Get ready to unlock the secrets of financial independence, and let the adventure begin!

No wand waving needed—just practical steps to help beginners like you take control of your money and pave the way for a future of financial freedom. Let's unravel the secrets to managing personal finances and setting yourself on the path to financial independence!

Step 1: Enchanting Budget Mastery

Your journey begins with enchanting budget mastery. Picture your budget as a map that guides you through the financial landscape. Start by listing your sources of income, whether it's an allowance, gifts, or money earned from chores. Next, map out your monthly expenses, distinguishing between needs (like food and shelter) and wants (like the latest magical gadgets). The goal is to ensure your spending aligns with your income, leaving a little extra for savings and adventures.

Step 2: Spellbinding Savings Techniques

Now that you've mastered budget enchantment, it's time to delve into spellbinding savings techniques. Imagine your savings as magical seeds you plant for future growth. Begin by setting a savings goal—it could be for a special purchase, an emergency fund, or even a future quest like education. Create a savings jar or open a magical savings account to keep your treasures safe. Consistently watering these seeds with small amounts regularly will yield a bountiful financial garden over time.

Step 3: Shielding Your Gold: The Importance of Insurance

In the enchanted world of personal finances, unexpected twists can occur. That's where shielding your gold with insurance comes in. Explore the different types of insurance spells, such as health insurance for magical healing, and understand how they protect your finances from unexpected surprises. Having the right insurance shields in place ensures that you can brave any financial storm with confidence.

Step 4: Investing Magic: Growing Your Wealth

Now, let's unlock the secrets of investing magic to grow your wealth over time. Investing is like planting seeds in the financial garden, expecting them to flourish into mighty trees. Begin with simple investments, such as a magical piggy bank or a beginner's investment account. Learn about stocks, bonds, and mutual funds—these are the magical tools that can turn your small contributions into powerful financial spells over the years.

Step 5: Debt Disenchantment: Taming the Borrowing Dragon

Beware the borrowing dragon! Debt can be a formidable foe on the path to financial independence. Your mission is to practice debt disenchantment by understanding the difference between good and bad debt. Good debt might include a loan for education, while bad debt could be from impulsive purchases. Tame the borrowing dragon by prioritizing the repayment of bad debt, ensuring it doesn't hinder your magical financial journey.

Step 6: Financial Learning Quests: Lifelong Education

As a budding financial maestro, embark on lifelong learning quests to deepen your understanding of personal finances. Explore books, attend workshops, and seek guidance from experienced mentors. The more you learn, the more empowered you become in making wise financial decisions. Think of it as unlocking new spells and enchantments to bolster your financial arsenal.

Step 7: Magical Money Partnerships: Seek Wise Counsel

No sorcerer is an island, and the same applies to managing personal finances. Forge magical money partnerships by seeking wise counsel from financial advisors, mentors, or knowledgeable family members. Their guidance can provide valuable insights, helping you navigate the complexities of the financial realm.

While we won't be conjuring spells or waving wands, we'll delve into practical steps and strategies that will empower you to take control of your money. Get ready to unlock the secrets of financial independence, and let the adventure begin!

The Enchanted Path to Financial Independence

Imagine financial independence as a distant land filled with opportunities and adventures. Your journey begins by walking the enchanted path of managing personal finances. Together, we'll navigate this path, learning essential skills that will serve as your compass on the road to financial freedom.

Chapter Toolkit: Your Guide to Financial Mastery

Before we set off, let's familiarize ourselves with the tools you'll need for this quest. Think of them as your magical toolkit:

1. Budget Wand: This tool will help you cast spells of budget mastery, ensuring your income and expenses dance in harmony.
2. Savings Amulet: Harness the power of savings to create a magical amulet that will protect you from unexpected twists in your financial tale.
3. Insurance Shield: Craft a shield of insurance to guard against unforeseen challenges, ensuring your financial fortress remains strong.

4. Investment Crystal Ball: Peer into the investment crystal ball to understand how your money can grow over time through wise investment choices.
5. Debt Disenchantment Elixir: Brew a powerful elixir to disenchant debts, ensuring they don't cast a shadow on your path to financial independence.
6. Learning Grimoire: Open the learning grimoire to absorb financial wisdom from various sources, enhancing your understanding of personal finance.
7. Counselor's Quill: Seek guidance with the counselor's quill, reaching out to wise mentors or advisors who can illuminate your financial journey.

Mapping Your Financial Landscape

The first step on your journey is to map your financial landscape. Picture your income streams, whether from chores, allowances, or gifts, as the fertile ground. Next, identify your monthly expenses—the rivers and hills that shape your financial terrain. Mapping this landscape will give you a clear view of where your money comes from and where it goes.

Casting Budget Spells

With your budget wand in hand, it's time to cast budget spells. Break down your expenses into categories like necessities (food, shelter) and non-essentials (entertainment, treats). Channel your inner financial wizard to ensure that your spending aligns with your income, leaving room for savings and investments.

Conjuring the Savings Amulet

Now, let's conjure the savings amulet. Set a savings goal—it could be for a magical item you've been eyeing or an emergency fund for unexpected quests. Regularly contribute to your savings amulet, and watch it grow into a powerful force that provides financial security.

Crafting the Insurance Shield

As you continue your journey, craft the insurance shield to protect against unforeseen challenges. Explore different insurance spells, such as health and home insurance, to fortify your defenses. An insurance shield ensures that unexpected storms won't disrupt your path to financial independence.

Gazing into the Investment Crystal Ball

Peering into the investment crystal ball, you'll discover the magic of growing your wealth. Learn about stocks, bonds, and other investment enchantments. By making informed choices, you can watch your money multiply and work for you over time.

Brewing the Debt Disenchantment Elixir

No financial wizard wants to be entangled by the borrowing dragon. Brew the debt disenchantment elixir by understanding the types of debt and prioritizing their repayment. This powerful potion ensures that bad debt doesn't cast a shadow on your magical financial journey.

Consulting the Learning Grimoire

Open the learning grimoire to enhance your financial wisdom. Explore books, online resources, and perhaps even financial quests in your community. The more spells you add to your financial repertoire, the more adept you become at managing your personal finances.

Seeking Wisdom with the Counselor's Quill

Your journey wouldn't be complete without seeking wisdom from the counselor's quill. Connect with mentors, advisors, or knowledgeable family members who can provide guidance on your financial path. Their insights can illuminate your way, helping you navigate challenges and seize opportunities.

As we conclude this chapter on managing personal finances, remember that your journey to financial independence is an ongoing adventure. Armed with your enchanted toolkit, you're equipped to navigate the twists and turns of the financial realm. May your path be filled with wise budget spells, flourishing savings amulets, resilient insurance shields, prosperous investment crystal balls, potent debt disenchantment elixirs, a vast learning grimoire, and the guidance of the counselor's quill.

19

GLOBAL ECONOMICS: CURRENCY EXCHANGE AND INTERNATIONAL FINANCE

We're setting sail to discover the wonders of currency exchange, international finance, and the incredible dance of money on the world stage. Get ready to don your explorer hat, as we navigate the high seas of global finance and uncover the mysteries that make the world go 'round!

Imagine a treasure map that spans the entire globe—that's what currency exchange is all about! We'll unravel the secrets of how different countries use unique currencies, each with its own magical value. From dollars to euros, yen to pesos, understanding currency exchange is like deciphering the codes to unlock treasures from around the world.

Step 1: Cracking the Currency Code

Our first stop on this global adventure is cracking the currency code. Learn the symbols and codes that represent currencies—it's like learning the magical language of money. Whether it's the dollar sign ($) or the euro symbol (€), you'll soon be fluent in the international language of finance.

Step 2: The Magical Dance of Exchange Rates

Now, let's step onto the dance floor and join the magical dance of exchange rates. Exchange rates determine how much one currency is worth in another. Picture it as a lively dance where currencies cha-cha, tango, and waltz with each other. We'll explore how these rates change, influenced by economic factors, just like the tides of the ocean.

Step 3: Tales of Travel and Trade

Embark on tales of travel and trade as we explore how currency exchange impacts our global adventures. Imagine you're trading magical souvenirs from your homeland with a friend in a faraway land. How much are your treasures worth in their currency? Discover the joys and challenges of international trade and the importance of currency exchange in making it all possible.

The Global Bazaar: International Finance in Action

Now, let's stroll through the bustling marketplaces of the global bazaar, where international finance comes to life. From stocks and bonds to investments in different countries, the global bazaar is a vibrant hub of economic activity. We'll meet international investors, savvy traders, and financial wizards who navigate this lively marketplace with skill and flair.

Step 4: Stocking Up on Global Stocks

Ever thought about owning a piece of a company from another part of the world? That's where global stocks come into play! We'll embark on a quest to understand how stocks and investments can transcend borders. It's like collecting magical tokens from different regions, each contributing to your global portfolio of wealth.

Step 5: Navigating the Currency Market Maze

Picture the currency market as a maze filled with twists and turns. In this step, we'll become expert navigators, understanding how the currency market operates. From the bustling streets of Wall Street to the scenic byways of Tokyo, the currency market maze is where global currencies come to play. You'll soon be equipped to decipher its intricate pathways.

Step 6: Diplomacy in Dollars: The Role of Central Banks

Just as wizards have their councils, the world of finance has central banks. We'll explore the diplomatic role of central banks, the guardians of a country's currency. These financial wizards use spells like interest rates and monetary policies to keep their currencies stable and protect their economies from magical storms.

Ready your sails, for we're about to navigate uncharted waters and uncover more treasures of wisdom on this economic odyssey!

Step 7: Mastering the Art of Hedging

Imagine you're a seasoned captain steering your financial ship through unpredictable waters. That's the essence of mastering the art of hedging in international finance. Hedging is like having a magical compass that helps you navigate the highs and lows of the financial sea. Learn how businesses and investors use hedging strategies to shield themselves from unexpected storms and ensure smooth sailing.

Step 8: Tales from the Cryptocurrency Cove

Just when you thought the adventure couldn't get more exciting, we arrive at the mysterious Cryptocurrency Cove. Cryptocurrencies, like Bitcoin and Ethereum, are the hidden treasures of the digital realm. Explore how these magical currencies are changing the landscape of international finance and imagine a world where transactions happen with the click of a digital wand.

Step 9: Cultural Currency Customs

Every country has its own set of customs, and the same goes for currencies! Let's immerse ourselves in the cultural currency customs that shape financial interactions around the world. From bowing to the yen in Japan to exchanging pleasantries with the pound in the United Kingdom, understanding these customs adds a touch of cultural magic to our global financial voyage.

Picture the Great Economic Silk Road, a network of trade routes connecting lands far and wide. In this step, we'll explore how these trade routes of prosperity contribute to the global economic tapestry. From spices and silks in ancient times to goods and services in the modern era, the economic Silk Road has been a conduit for the exchange of wealth and ideas.

Step 10: Economic Crises

Just as seafarers face storms on the high seas, the world of international finance encounters economic crises. Explore the challenges posed by economic storms—from recessions to currency crises. Learn how countries navigate these turbulent waters and the role international cooperation plays in weathering financial tempests.

Step 11: A Global Financial Code of Ethics

In our quest for financial wisdom, let's uncover the global financial code of ethics. Discover the principles that guide ethical financial conduct on the international stage. It's like crafting a moral compass that ensures fair play, transparency, and responsible financial practices in the global economic community.

As we approach the final leg of our journey, let's explore the currency of compassion. Philanthropy on a global scale involves using financial resources to make a positive impact on communities worldwide. Whether it's funding education initiatives, supporting healthcare, or addressing environmental challenges, the currency of compassion has the power to create a more equitable and magical world.

Congratulations, Fearless Explorers! You've navigated the high seas of currency exchange and international finance, unlocking the secrets that make the global economic engine hum. As you continue your financial odyssey, remember that your passport is not just a document; it's a symbol of the knowledge and understanding you've gained on this adventure.

20

DIGITAL FINANCE: NAVIGATING ONLINE BANKING AND PAYMENT SYSTEMS

We're setting out to explore the wonders of online banking and payment systems, where technology meets finance in a magical fusion. Grab your virtual compass, as we navigate the digital landscape and uncover the secrets that make money move at the speed of light!

Imagine a gateway to a digital realm where your money is just a click away—that's the magic of online banking! In this section, we'll demystify the concept of online banking and explore how it transforms traditional financial activities into convenient, virtual experiences. Get ready to enter the world of 24/7 access, digital statements, and financial transactions at your fingertips.

The first step on our digital adventure is activating your digital portal—your gateway to online banking. Imagine it as a magical door that opens to a realm where your financial affairs are managed with ease. Learn how to set up your online banking account, secure it with virtual locks, and customize your digital space for a personalized financial experience.

As you navigate the digital landscape, security becomes your magical shield. Explore the spells of secure sorcery—password charms, two-factor authentication enchantments, and biometric incantations—that protect your online banking kingdom from digital dragons and mischievous wizards. Your digital fortress should be impenetrable, ensuring a safe and secure financial journey.

Now that your digital portal is secure, let's dive into the magic of money movements. Discover how to cast spells for transfers and transactions, whether you're sending money to a friend, paying bills, or making online purchases. The digital world allows you to move your money effortlessly, as if sending it on the wings of a digital phoenix.

Picture a magical wallet that holds not just coins and bills, but also your digital currency. We'll explore the concept of digital wallets, where technology and finance intertwine. Whether it's mobile payment apps, e-wallets, or contactless payments, your digital wallet is the key to unlocking a world where transactions happen with a wave or tap.

Embark on QR code quests and contactless adventures as we explore the magic of scanning codes and making payments without physical contact. It's like wielding a digital wand to cast spells that complete transactions seamlessly. Discover how technology has turned everyday activities into digital enchantments with the power of QR codes and contactless payments.

What if you could concoct potions and share them with friends digitally? That's the essence of peer-to-peer potion making, where you can transfer money directly to your friends with just a few taps. Explore the world of peer-to-peer payment apps and discover how they've revolutionized the way you share expenses, split bills, and send money to friends in the blink of an eye.

In the heart of digital finance lies the mysterious blockchain spell. Unravel the secrets of the digital ledger, a decentralized and tamper-resistant system that ensures the transparency and security of digital transactions. It's like having an enchanted scroll that records every financial transaction in a way that's both secure and transparent.

As you navigate the digital realm, meet your companions: budgeting apps that act as digital wizards. Discover how these apps, equipped with charts, graphs, and spending insights, can help you master the art of budgeting in the digital age. It's like having a financial mentor in your pocket, guiding you towards your financial goals.

Our journey through the digital finance landscape is far from over. In this next segment, we'll dive deeper into the sea of possibilities, exploring advanced features, futuristic trends, and the evolving magic of online banking and payment systems. So, buckle up, and let's sail into the uncharted waters of the digital financial horizon!

As we sail further into the digital realm, let's unlock the gates to advanced alchemy—investing in the digital era. Explore how online platforms and apps have transformed the way people invest. From digital investment platforms to robo-advisors, these tools can empower you to grow your wealth and make investment decisions with the precision of a digital sorcerer.

Cryptocurrencies are like the mysterious potions of the digital world. In this step, we'll decode the cryptocurrency conundrum. From Bitcoin to Ethereum, uncover the secrets of these digital coins, their decentralized nature, and the blockchain spells that make them secure. Imagine a world where you can buy, sell, and invest in digital currencies—welcome to the future of finance!

What if managing money became as fun as playing a game? Enter the realm of financial fitness challenges, where apps gamify money management. Learn how these platforms turn budgeting and saving into interactive quests, making financial responsibility an enjoyable adventure. It's like having a personal finance coach who speaks the language of gaming!

Picture an arcade where banking meets augmented reality—that's the magic of interactive banking experiences. As technology advances, augmented reality (AR) is transforming the way we interact with our finances. From virtual financial advisors to immersive banking simulations, step into the augmented reality arcade for a futuristic and interactive financial adventure.

In a world where your voice is the key, enter the voice-activated vault of banking with virtual assistants. Discover how technologies like Siri, Alexa, or Google Assistant can assist with banking transactions, account inquiries, and even financial advice. It's like having a personal finance assistant at your beck and call, responding to your financial wishes with just a vocal command.

As we conclude this segment, let's peer into the crystal ball of tomorrow's tech marvels. Anticipate future trends in digital finance, from artificial intelligence revolutionizing customer service to biometric authentication shaping the future of security. The digital landscape is ever-evolving, and staying ahead of the curve ensures you're ready for the financial adventures of the future.

Congratulations, Digital Navigators! You've delved into the depths of online banking and digital finance, uncovering the treasures that await in this magical realm. As your digital odyssey continues, may you boldly explore the frontiers of investing, navigate the cryptocurrency seas, conquer financial fitness challenges, and embrace the futuristic wonders that technology brings to finance. Onward, into the future of digital finance!

21

FINANCIAL WIZARDS UNLEASHED: BECOMING SCHOOL'S MONEY EXPERTS

Imagine wielding financial knowledge like a magical staff, enchanting your peers and teachers with your money mastery. Get ready to don your wizarding robes and embark on a journey to become the financial wizards your school needs!

Picture your school as a magical realm, and the corridors of learning as pathways to financial wisdom. In this section, we'll transform your school into the School of Financial Magic—a place where financial knowledge becomes a powerful spellbook, and you, the students, are the wizards-in-training.

Every wizard needs a toolkit, and yours will be brimming with financial instruments. From budgeting spells to investment enchantments, assemble your financial toolkit by gathering the knowledge and skills needed to become a true money maestro. Imagine it as a magical backpack filled with tools to solve financial puzzles and cast spells of financial mastery.

In your journey to become a financial wizard, seek guidance from the Financial Sorcerer's Apprentice—teachers, mentors, or even professionals with expertise in finance. Attend workshops, engage in discussions, and absorb the wisdom they share. Your apprenticeship will be a transformative experience, honing your financial skills under the watchful eye of those who have mastered the art.

It's time to step onto the stage as the spell-crafting sorcerer. Organize workshops and presentations to share your financial knowledge with fellow students. Imagine it as a magical seminar where you illuminate the secrets of budgeting, saving, and investing. With each workshop, you're not just sharing spells—you're empowering your peers to become financial wizards in their own right.

What if your school hosted a Financial Fair, a bustling marketplace of financial knowledge? Organize booths, demonstrations, and interactive sessions to showcase your wizardry to the entire school. Picture it as a grand spectacle where students, teachers, and even parents gather to witness the magic of financial empowerment.

To amplify your magical influence, consider forming a Financial Wizard Guild—a club where aspiring financial wizards gather to share knowledge and expertise. As guild members, you'll collaborate on projects, organize events, and support each other on your journey to financial mastery. Together, you'll create a community of financial wizards making a positive impact in your school.

Turn your school into a realm of financial quests and challenges. Organize fun and interactive activities that engage the entire school in financial adventures. From budgeting challenges to investment simulations, these quests will not only entertain but also impart valuable financial lessons to all who participate.

Imagine chronicling your financial adventures in a magical tome—"The Financial Chronicles." Create a platform, whether it's a blog, newsletter, or video series, to document and share your financial insights. By publishing your wizardry, you're not just building your legacy but also inspiring others to embark on their own financial journeys.

Our journey to become the money experts of your school continues. In this next segment, let's delve into more advanced magical practices, from organizing financial events to collaborating with your fellow wizards. Together, let's amplify your financial influence and truly unleash the wizardry within you.

Step 1: Magical Financial Events

Elevate your financial wizardry by hosting magical financial events such as seminars and symposiums. Envision the school auditorium transformed into a grand hall of knowledge, where you and your fellow wizards share advanced financial spells. From investment strategies to understanding economic trends, these events will leave a lasting impact on your peers and teachers.

Step 2: Collaborative Spellcasting

Imagine a magical tournament where financial wizards from different schools gather to showcase their skills. Collaborate with other schools to organize inter-school competitions. It's not just a battle of spells but a collaborative effort to elevate financial literacy across the magical realm of education. Competitions can include quizzes, debates, and innovative financial projects.

Transform financial wisdom into an art form by creating a Financial Art Gallery. Visualize the walls adorned with paintings, illustrations, and multimedia displays that convey financial concepts and lessons. Through artistic expression, you'll engage students in a creative exploration of money matters, making financial education both enjoyable and enlightening.

Step 3: Spreading Financial News

Become the editors of *The Financial Gazette*, a magical publication that spreads financial news and insights throughout your school. Envision a school newspaper or digital platform where you and your fellow wizards curate articles, interviews, and features on relevant financial topics. This publication will serve as a beacon, enlightening your school community with the latest in financial wisdom.

Step 4: Mentorship Magic

As seasoned financial wizards, it's time to extend your guidance to junior wizards-in-training. Envision a mentorship program where you share your knowledge and experiences with younger students. Through one-on-one sessions, workshops, or even a financial buddy system, you'll foster a culture of continuous learning and mentorship within your school.

Cap off your magical year by hosting the Grand Financial Feast, an event that celebrates the achievements and financial growth of your school community. Picture it as a banquet where financial wizards, teachers, and students come together to reflect on their financial journey. Share success stories, recognize accomplishments, and set the stage for a future filled with continued financial wizardry.

22

ADVANCED MONEY MANAGEMENT: STRATEGIES FOR SUCCESS

Step right up, young financial enthusiasts, to the most exciting event under the financial big top—the Money Mastery Carnival!

Welcome to a chapter like no other, where the world of advanced money management transforms into a whimsical carnival of financial wisdom and fun. Picture a lively carnival atmosphere filled with games, laughter, and, most importantly, valuable lessons on mastering your money.

In this thrilling chapter, we invite you to explore the carnival grounds where financial strategies take center stage. The Money Mastery Carnival is not just about learning; it's about experiencing the exhilaration of advanced money management in a way that's both entertaining and educational.

As you venture through the carnival games, each one designed to unveil the secrets of financial success, you'll discover the joy of budgeting through balloon pops, the strategic thrill of investment ring toss, and the excitement of navigating the Wheel of Credit Fortune. Get ready to topple the Investment Jenga Tower, take risks in the Dunk Tank, and unravel tax mysteries in the Tax Tumble Funhouse.

But it's not all fun and games—each carnival attraction is carefully crafted to impart advanced money management strategies. So, buckle up for a financial rollercoaster that combines the excitement of the carnival with the knowledge that will empower you to navigate the complexities of your financial journey.

So, grab your tickets, embark on this financial adventure, and let the Money Mastery Carnival begin! It's time to enjoy the ride and master your money with a smile on your face and a pocket full of financial wisdom.

Game 1:

The Budget Balloon Pop

Picture a field filled with colorful budget balloons—each representing a spending category. Your mission? Pop the balloons strategically to reveal budget allocations. This game turns budgeting into a lively carnival experience. With each pop, you'll unveil the secrets to allocating funds for essentials, savings, and even a sprinkle of fun money!

Game 2:

Investment Ring Toss

Step up to the Investment Ring Toss, where financial instruments are the rings waiting to be tossed onto the investment targets. From stocks to bonds, aim for the highest returns as you learn the art of diversified investments. It's not just a game; it's an investment strategy extravaganza that hones your skills in building a robust investment portfolio.

Game 3:

Wheel of Credit Fortune

Take a spin on the Wheel of Credit Fortune, a mesmerizing carnival wheel filled with credit scenarios. Will you land on the "Smart Credit Moves" or the "Credit Pitfall"? Learn advanced credit management strategies as you navigate the twists and turns of the credit wheel, avoiding traps and making savvy financial decisions.

Game 4:

Risky Business Dunk Tank

Ever dreamt of dunking risk into a tank of financial wisdom? Well, step right up to the Risky Business Dunk Tank! Toss financial risks into the tank, and with each successful dunk, uncover risk mitigation strategies. Whether it's emergency funds, insurance, or strategic planning, this game teaches you how to keep your financial ship afloat in turbulent waters.

Game 5:

Investment Jenga Tower

Brace yourself for the Investment Jenga Tower, a towering structure of financial opportunities and risks. Strategically pull out blocks labeled with investment decisions, and watch the tower grow or wobble. This game transforms investment planning into a thrilling Jenga experience, where each move teaches you the delicate balance of risk and reward.

Game 6:

Tax Tumble Funhouse

Enter the Tax Tumble Funhouse, a kaleidoscope of tax scenarios and deductions. Navigate through the twists and turns of tax laws, deductions, and credits as you emerge from the funhouse with a clearer understanding of advanced tax planning strategies. It's not just a ride; it's a tax-tastic adventure!

Game 7:

Financial Escape Room Extravaganza

Prepare for the Financial Escape Room Extravaganza, where you and your friends collaborate to solve financial puzzles and unlock the secrets to financial success. From decoding investment clues to budgeting riddles, this game tests your mastery of advanced money management strategies in an immersive and interactive setting.

Each game was designed not just to entertain but to impart advanced money management strategies in a way that's engaging and memorable. May your financial journey continue to be a thrilling carnival ride filled with financial success and, of course, heaps of fun!

23

ENTREPRENEURIAL EXCELLENCE: TAKING BUSINESS VENTURES TO NEW HEIGHTS

Envision your entrepreneurial journey as a blank canvas, awaiting the strokes of your creativity and the hues of your vision. The Entrepreneurial Canvas is where ideas flourish, dreams take shape, and the pursuit of excellence begins. As we dive into this chapter, let this canvas be your playground, where you'll paint the vibrant landscape of your entrepreneurial venture.

The stage is set, and the spotlight is on you. In the Ideation Illumination chamber, we'll explore the spark of creativity that ignites groundbreaking ideas. From there, Blueprint Brilliance lays the groundwork for turning your vision into a tangible business plan. This is where dreams start to morph into strategic realities, setting the course for entrepreneurial success.

Leadership is the heartbeat of entrepreneurship. As you step into the Leadership Laboratory, envision honing the skills that define a true entrepreneurial leader—someone who not only charts a course but inspires and guides a team toward a common goal. The Entrepreneurial Playground is where leadership becomes an art, propelling your venture forward with purpose and direction.

Feel the anticipation in the air as we move from the drawing board to the real world. The Launchpad to Launch phase catapults your venture into the market, introducing your product or service to eager audiences. It's a moment of excitement, strategy, and the first taste of how your entrepreneurial vision resonates with the world.

The path to entrepreneurial excellence is dotted with challenges and unexpected turns. Picture the Resilience Reservoir as your source of strength, a reservoir that replenishes your resolve when faced with setbacks. Here, we'll delve into the art of resilience, guiding you through the unpredictable terrains of entrepreneurship with adaptability and fortitude.

In the Innovation Oasis, witness the continuous evolution of your venture. Here, innovation is not just a buzzword; it's the lifeblood of sustained growth. Explore how embracing change, staying ahead of trends, and fostering a culture of innovation can keep your entrepreneurial oasis thriving in a dynamic market.

As your venture gains momentum, Scaling Summits becomes the next chapter. This phase is about reaching new heights, expanding your reach, and conquering entrepreneurial summits. Picture it as the ascent to success, where strategic scaling transforms your business from a venture to a formidable presence in the market.

As we wrap up our magical journey through Entrepreneurial Excellence, it's time to distill the wizardry of business into lessons fit for the youngest dreamers and creators. Just as wizards cast spells to make magic, entrepreneurs cast ideas to make dreams come true. So, let's sprinkle a bit of enchantment on our entrepreneurial odyssey.

Imagine you're the Dream Weaver, conjuring ideas that shimmer with possibility. Whether it's a flying car, a robot friend, or a cookie-making machine, your dreams are the seeds of your entrepreneurial journey. Now, let's take those dreams and turn them into a magical blueprint, a treasure map guiding you to the heart of your imaginative ventures.

So, what are you still waiting for?

24

BEYOND SCHOOL: PRACTICAL FINANCIAL LESSONS FOR EVERYDAY LIFE

As we step beyond the familiar walls of school, a new adventure awaits us in the realm of practical financial lessons for everyday life. This chapter is your compass to navigate the intricacies of personal finance, transforming theoretical knowledge into practical skills that empower you to make informed financial decisions in the real world.

Lesson 1: The Currency of Daily Choices

Picture your daily choices as currency—a precious resource to spend wisely. From the morning decision of choosing breakfast to evening choices like entertainment or study time, understand the value each choice holds. This lesson teaches you to budget your daily choices wisely, ensuring a healthy balance between wants and needs.

Lesson 2: The Savings Sanctuary

Imagine creating a Savings Sanctuary, a magical place where your money grows and multiplies. Learn the art of saving, setting aside a portion of your allowance or earnings for the future. With the Savings Sanctuary, you'll build a financial fortress that shields you from unexpected storms and opens doors to future opportunities.

Lesson 3: The Grocery Store Expedition

Embark on a Grocery Store Expedition, a mission to discover the secrets of smart shopping. Navigate the aisles with a budget-conscious mindset, distinguishing between needs and wants. Picture yourself as the captain of your shopping cart, steering clear of financial pitfalls and making choices that nourish both your health and your wallet.

Lesson 4: The Bill Paying Adventure

As you transition to managing your own finances, embark on the Bill Paying Adventure. Envision it as a quest where you conquer bills and expenses like a financial hero. Learn the importance of paying bills on time, budgeting for utilities, and mastering the art of responsible financial management. This adventure ensures a smooth journey through the fiscal landscape.

Lesson 5: The Credit and Debit Duel

Enter the Credit and Debit Duel, a friendly battle between these two financial allies. Understand the differences between credit and debit, envisioning them as trusty companions on your financial journey. Learn to use them wisely, avoiding the pitfalls of debt and building a positive financial history from a young age.

Lesson 6: The Investment Playground

Picture the Investment Playground, a space where your money plays and grows over time. Dive into the world of investments, exploring concepts like stocks, bonds, and mutual funds. This lesson teaches you to become a wise player on the Investment Playground, making informed decisions that contribute to your long-term financial goals.

Lesson 7: The Insurance Fortress

As you build your financial fortress, don the armor of the Insurance Fortress. Envision it as a protective shield against unexpected challenges. Learn about different types of insurance—from health to property—and understand how they safeguard your financial well-being. This lesson ensures that you're prepared for unexpected storms that may come your way.

Lesson 8: The Charity Quest

Embark on the Charity Quest, a noble journey where you use your financial knowledge to make a positive impact on the world. Imagine yourself as a philanthropic hero, contributing to causes you care about. This lesson instills the importance of giving back and making a difference in the lives of others through thoughtful and purposeful giving.

Congratulations, Everyday Explorers, on completing this journey through the practical landscape of personal finance! You've acquired a treasure trove of knowledge that will serve as your compass in the uncharted territory of everyday financial decisions. As you set forth into the world beyond school, remember that each choice you make, whether big or small, is an opportunity to apply these lessons and shape your financial destiny.

Consider this chapter not as an endpoint but as a launchpad for your ongoing financial expedition. The skills you've gained—budgeting, saving, smart shopping, bill management, understanding credit and investments, securing your financial fortress with insurance, and embracing the spirit of giving—will be the guiding stars of your financial journey.

Visualize your financial future as a canvas waiting for your unique strokes. With each stroke, you paint a picture of financial independence, resilience, and success. Your Savings Sanctuary, Investment Playground, and Insurance Fortress will stand as pillars of strength, supporting you through the chapters of your life.

As you move forward, take pride in your ability to make informed choices that align with your values and aspirations. Whether you're crafting a budget, deciding where to invest, or contributing to a charitable cause, remember that your financial decisions echo the values you hold dear.

In closing, let the wisdom gained from this chapter be your eternal companion. May your financial expedition be filled with smart choices, financial victories, and a legacy of positive impact.

25

EQUIPPED FOR A LIFETIME OF FINANCIAL MASTERY

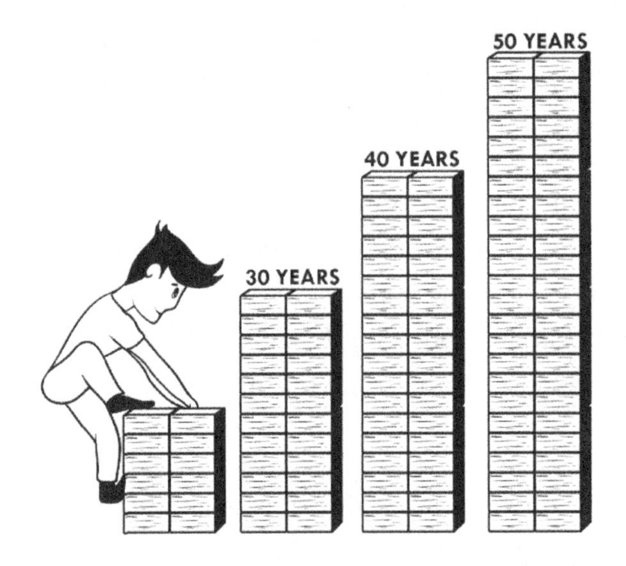

Hey, Money Wizards in the making!

Imagine this chapter as the grand finale of your adventure into the land of money knowledge. You've explored the secrets of dollars and cents, and now you're loaded with the tools, smarts, and confidence to handle money like a champ for the rest of your life.

Think of your money toolkit like a treasure chest full of things to help you succeed. In this chapter, we're going to open it up and show you what's inside. Each tool in there is like a skill or idea that will help you be awesome with your money. From planning and saving to investing and giving back, these tools are your secret weapons for becoming a money master.

Tool 1: The Spending Plan Stick

Imagine having a magical Spending Plan Stick that lets you control your money super well. This tool helps you make a plan for how you'll spend your money, making sure you use it wisely. With the Spending Plan Stick, you get to be the boss of your money.

Tool 2: The Savings Super Shield

Picture a Savings Super Shield that keeps you safe from unexpected money troubles. This shield is made by saving money regularly, building a strong money fortress that protects your dreams. With the Savings Super Shield, you're ready to face any money challenges that come your way.

Tool 3: The Growing Money Key

Think of the Growing Money Key as a special key that opens the door to the Money Growing Playground. This key helps you make smart choices about making your money grow over time. As you play around with your money in the Money Growing Playground, the Growing Money Key makes sure you make clever decisions.

As we dig deeper into your money toolkit, let's uncover more magical tools that will make you a true master of money. Picture each tool as a friendly sidekick, ready to assist you on your journey to financial mastery.

Tool 4: The Wise Choices Crown

Imagine placing the Wise Choices Crown on your head—a symbol of making smart decisions with your money. This tool helps you choose wisely between what you really need and what might just be a want. With the Wise Choices Crown, you become the king or queen of sensible spending.

Tool 5: The Give Back Cape

Envision putting on the Give Back Cape, a special cape that turns you into a superhero of generosity. This tool teaches you about giving back and making a positive impact on the world. With the Give Back Cape, you have the power to share your good fortune and spread kindness wherever you go.

Tool 6: The Learn More Lens

Think of the Learn More Lens as a pair of magical glasses that help you see opportunities to grow your money knowledge. This tool encourages you to keep learning about money and discover new ways to make it work for you. With the Learn More Lens, you're equipped to stay curious and informed throughout your financial journey.

Tool 7: The Share Smarts Scepter

Hold up the Share Smarts Scepter, a magical stick that encourages you to share your money wisdom with others. This tool reminds you that helping friends or family understand money can make everyone's journey a little bit easier. With the Share Smarts Scepter, you become a money mentor, spreading your knowledge far and wide.

Tool 8: The Future Explorer Map

Imagine unfolding the Future Explorer Map, a magical map that guides you toward your money dreams. This tool helps you set goals, plan for the future, and navigate the exciting unknowns of your financial journey. With the Future Explorer Map, you're ready to turn your dreams into real-life adventures.

As we conclude this chapter on being ready for a lifetime of money smarts, see yourself as the hero of your money story. With each tool in your toolkit, you've gained a new superpower to conquer challenges, make wise choices, and create a future filled with financial success.

Remember, this isn't the end of your money adventure—it's just the beginning. Armed with your magical toolkit, you're now on a quest for a lifetime of money mastery. So, go forth, young money wizard, and may your financial journey be filled with prosperity, wisdom, and a sprinkle of magic!

CONCLUSION

Dear Money Adventurers,

You've embarked on a remarkable journey through the magical realms of financial wisdom, and we hope the lessons learned have left you empowered, inspired, and ready to face the exciting adventures that lie ahead.

In this epilogue, we want to take a moment to reflect on the incredible path you've traveled. From the basic foundations of money to the advanced concepts of investments and entrepreneurship, you've delved into the enchanted world of financial literacy. Each chapter was crafted with the intention of making complex ideas accessible, relatable, and, most importantly, fun for young minds like yours.

As you venture forth, we encourage you to stay curious, keep learning, and embrace the joy of mastering your money. Share your wisdom with those around you, and remember that financial mastery is not just about the numbers; it's about the choices you make and the dreams you strive to achieve.

Thank you for joining us on this magical expedition. May your future be filled with financial success, endless possibilities, and a touch of enchantment. Here's to the end of one adventure and the exciting beginning of many more.

SPECIAL BONUS

Want this bonus book for free?

SKILLS and be the first to claim a free download of our upcoming releases.

Scan the QR CODE

Join Today!

THANK YOU

Thank you for choosing our resource to suppor[t] your child's growth; it means so much to us.

If you could take a moment to share your thoughts o[n] Amazon or Goodreads.com, it would mean a lot to u[s] and be a great help to other parents searching for trusted resources. Thank you.

Want to dive into the literary world before anyone else? Then join our Book Launch Club! As a club member, you'll be offered the opportunity to receive advanced copies of our upcoming releases directly to your inbox. All we ask is for you to leave honest reviews on Amazon.com and Goodreads.com. Your honest feedback will contribute to the book's success and help fellow readers make informed choices.

For more information on joining Skilled Fun's Book Launch Club skilledfun.com/book-launch-club or simply scan our QR CODE

Made in United States
North Haven, CT
13 June 2025

69788577R00085